THE CULTURALLY CUSTOMIZED WEB SITE

Customizing Web Sites for the Global Marketplace

ELSEVIER
BUTTERWORTH
HEINEMANN

Nitish Singh, Ph.D.
California State University, Chico

Arun Pereira, Ph.D.
Saint Louis University

Elsevier Butterworth–Heinemann
30 Corporate Drive, Suite 400, Burlington, MA 01803, USA
Linacre House, Jordan Hill, Oxford OX2 8DP, UK

 Recognizing the importance of preserving what has been written, Elsevier prints its books on
acid-free paper whenever possible.

Library of Congress Cataloging-in-Publication Data

On file at Library of Congress

British Library Cataloguing-in-Publication Data
A catalogue record for this book is available from the British Library.

ISBN: 0-7506-7849-6

For information on all Elsevier Butterworth–Heinemann publications
visit our Web site at www.books.elsevier.com

05   06   07   08   09   10   10 9 8 7 6 5 4 3 2 1

Printed in China

*For adoptive families the world over, in appreciation;
for Kavita and Meera, with love.*

-AP

CONTENTS

PREFACE

This book is the result of over four years of research on various aspects of e-commerce, culture, and online consumer behavior. The Internet, with its unparalleled access to global customers and the potential for highly-customized marketing, has brought with it both promise and peril for international marketers. The promise of being "born global" with access to far-flung customers at unprecedented low costs must be tempered with the need for extraordinary business savvy to effectively confront the complexity of international competition and pressure on profit margins. How a global marketer manages the access to a vast, multicultural customer base, and handles other competitors vying for these customers will determine if it succeeds in the marketplace.

A key issue in the quest for global success through the Internet is the ability to design a web site that draws targeted customers, generates the desired behavior (be it a purchase or otherwise), builds trust and loyalty with these customers, and is invulnerable to competitive marketing actions. The process for this will obviously vary, depending on the needs of the targeted customers—and customers in the global marketplace are of every cultural stripe possible, making for a multicultural sea of differing tastes and needs. In this context, where does one start to design web sites that are customized to draw specific cultural segments? The answer: right here, in this book.

Our research—along with the research of others—has emphatically shown that culturally-adapted web content enhances usability, accessibility, and web site interactivity, with the relevant cultural group. To help implement such cultural adaptation, we provide a theoretically-sound, rigorously-tested framework. This framework provides the fundamental steps needed to culturally customize web sites. Our approach is country-based; as such we assume that countries can be defined by their dominant culture. The key reason for such an approach is a practical one: At present, global businesses continue to use "countries" as a basis for segmenting and targeting global customers (e.g., companies talk in terms of "entering the Chinese market"). However, we recognize that the continuing march of globalization is dramatically changing the world with massive migrations of people, and national borders being redefined or erased. In this context, targeting countries must be done with caution; a country may have strong subcultures established by immigrants (for example, Indians in UK, French in Canada, etc.). However, it must be noted that the resulting situation—although more complex—is still structurally unchanged (targeting Canada may mean a secondary target of the French in Canada; thus both are again, "country" based). As such, our approach of defining countries based on their dominant culture(s) is practical, and readily implemented by companies looking for success in the global marketplace.

In conclusion, we would like to acknowledge the help and inspiration we received from faculty members and students at California State University and Saint Louis University. Our special thanks to California State University Research Foundation for the grant that they made available to write this book. Finally, we also extend our thanks to several academic reviewers and consultants that provided us valuable feedback and recommendations.

All examples of web sites used in the book were accessed from the Web during 2004. Please visit www.theculturallycustomizedwebsite.com for additional information and updates.

Nitish Singh
California State University, Chico
Arun Pereira
Saint Louis University

FOREWORD

The phenomenal growth of the Internet—and its associated World Wide Web—is a development that's not expected to abate in the near future. The World Wide Web removes all national boundaries in global commerce. With the expansion of market boundaries comes a broadening of the diversity within the pool of prospective customers. Thus, sales tools—such as web sites—must be treated with sensitivity to the demographic profiles of the various targets around the world. Companies that realize the importance of cultural differences, and design web materials with this in mind, will increase international market share—at the expense of those who ignore local customs. This book will help companies avoid unintended mistakes and cultural misunderstandings.

The Culturally Customized Web Site, by Professors Nitish Singh and Arun Pereira, is a timely publication that provides valuable information and insight into designing web sites for worldwide e-commerce. This book is the first comprehensive "how to" publication for customizing web sites to specific country cultures. The guidelines offered, which are specific and clearly written, are based on sound theory and vigorous empirical testing. Furthermore, this book is well organized, so that readers will easily understand the cultural differences underlying the global market.

Companies and institutions targeting culturally diverse customers can use this book to gain knowledge of the specific attributes required in a web site to attract a particular target group—increasing the probability of repeat visits and the building of customer trust and loyalty. For example, if a company wants to target customers in Australia, France, India, and China, the web sites will have to be different; reflecting core cultural differences which impact business practices and human behavior.

This book is appropriate for several audiences: First, web designers who design web sites for international companies and organizations will find that this book complements their technical expertise by offering insights into cultural diversity and its implications for web design. Second, managers of multinational companies and other organizations who target multicultural groups across the globe will find that this book provides a framework that will help them understand the breadth and depth of resources needed to be allocated in order to fund the cultural customization of their web materials. Finally, faculty who teach courses such as International Marketing, Global E-Commerce, International Advertising and other international business courses will find that this book provides an outline to teach students the cultural aspects of on-line marketing, based on established theory and empirical testing, along with end of chapter exercises that enhance the classroom learning experience.

The Boeing Institute of International Business at the Saint Louis University's John Cook School of Business offers both academic and professional programs in international business. The academic activities incorporate international business degree programs at the undergraduate, master and Ph.D. levels. The professional programs include global seminars, conferences, a data center, newsletters, and status as the publisher of the Multinational Business Review—an academic journal for business practitioners.

I am both happy and proud that Professor Singh and Professor Pereira have an intellectual and professional relationship with the Boeing Institute of International Business at the John Cook School of Business, Saint Louis University. Professor Singh received his Ph.D. degree through us and Professor Pereira has been teaching International Marketing and International Market Research, through the Boeing Institute of International Business, for years. It is gratifying to see our colleagues write a book that is at the forefront of an emerging area of international business and worldwide e-commerce.

Seung H. Kim, Ph.D.
Director and Professor of International Business
Boeing Institute of International Business
John Cook School of Business
Saint Louis University

CULTURE: THE NEW IMPERATIVE IN WEB DESIGN

This chapter introduces the changing face of global e-commerce and highlights the challenges involved in designing web sites that attract customers and foster trust and loyalty. Cultural customization of web sites is shown to be a necessary pre-requisite to building lasting relationships with diverse global customers.

CHAPTER HIGHLIGHTS

NEW CHALLENGES FOR WEB SITES

TRENDS IN E-COMMERCE

STANDARDIZATION VERSUS LOCALIZATION ON THE WEB

THE STATE OF WEB SITE CUSTOMIZATION

A CLASSIFICATION OF WEB SITES

WEB SITE CUSTOMIZATION: A STUDY

CULTURAL CUSTOMIZATION: THE NEXT IMPERATIVE IN WEB DESIGN

NEW CHALLENGES FOR WEB SITES

The World Wide Web is evolving to be the new frontier in international business, as it provides unprecedented advantages to companies attempting to tap the global market. In the past, size and the financial strength of a company were critical competitive advantages in reaching global consumers. Today, the Web allows companies of all sizes *instant* global reach and the *immediate* ability to interact with customers all over the world.

This is possible because the Internet provides unique efficiencies for companies attempting to conduct international business: it reduces advertising and communication costs in serving global market segments, allows for direct and easy access to customers and customer feedback, and reduces the need for intermediaries. However, these advantages often come with a price: a likely flood of competitors, all exploiting the same advantages, vying for the same target markets.

For customers, this means the availability of a wide choice of alternatives and unprecedented access to product information, enabling better-informed purchase decisions. For companies, this means pressure on prices and profit margins. More specifically, companies are likely to find revenue and profit growth challenging because low entry barriers on the Internet encourage the proliferation of competitors, adversely impacting customer-drawing power, pricing power as well as repeat buying, and customer loyalty. This is true regardless of whether the web site is a stand-alone entity (e.g., *www.Amazon.com*) or the online presence of an existing brand (e.g., *www.Honda.com*). In either case, unless a concerted effort is made to build a web site to thwart these market forces and foster customer trust and loyalty, the site will be doomed to mediocrity at best or failure at worst.

The Internet and the World Wide Web

The *Internet* is a massive network of networks, a networking infrastructure. It connects millions of computers together globally, forming a network in which any computer can communicate with any other computer as long as they are both connected to the Internet. Information that travels over the Internet does so via a variety of languages known as protocols.

The *World Wide Web*, or simply *Web*, is a way of accessing information over the medium of the Internet. It is an information-sharing model that is built on top of the Internet. The Web uses the HTTP protocol, only one of the languages spoken over the Internet, to transmit data. Web services, which use HTTP to allow applications to communicate in order to exchange business logic, use the Web to share information. The Web also utilizes browsers, such as Internet Explorer or Netscape, to access Web documents called Web pages that are linked to each other via hyperlinks. Web documents also contain graphics, sounds, text, and video.

The Web is just one of the ways that information can be disseminated over the Internet. The Internet, not the Web, is also used for e-mail, which relies on SMTP, Usenet news groups, instant messaging, and FTP. (Copyright, 2004 Jupitermedia All rights reserved. Reprinted with permission from www.internet.com. Source: www.webopedia.com/DidYouKnow/Internet/2002/Web_vs_Internet.asp)

Designing such a web site—one that draws customers, builds trust and loyalty, and is invulnerable to competitive marketing actions—is akin to *branding* the web site. After all, a successful brand enjoys exactly the same type of characteristics. As such, web sites that aim for success in the global marketplace must understand the lessons of branding, regardless of whether they are stand-alone entities like *www.ebay.com* (where it is necessary to build a brand from scratch) or online arms of existing brands like *www.pepsi.com* (where the objective is to sustain and enhance the existing brand).

Building a brand is a complex endeavor (see Keller 1998) for a comprehensive overview of branding) with no guarantee of success; however, what all successful brands have in common is a *customized and dynamic marketing strategy*. Such a strategy entails the continuous customization of marketing elements to the changing needs of a target market, sustained over time; this includes a unique product that adapts to changing market conditions, an integrated marketing communications program, and effective pricing and distribution.

A customized and dynamic marketing strategy will more likely lead to a successful brand if the brand in question is the first to enter the market—the market pioneer. Called *the first-mover advantage*, it is the advantage gained by the pioneer when it exploits its initial monopoly in the market to build a distinctive identity and establish customer loyalty, leading to long-term success that is unmatched by later entrants.

First-Mover Advantage

There is a large body of research that suggests that market pioneers ("first movers") have the potential to reap substantial rewards such as brand identity, customer loyalty, and market share leadership. However, much of this field of research has been called to question (e.g., see Tellis, Golder, and Christensen 2001); regardless, it can be said that first-movers have potential advantages—that may or may not be realized, depending on a variety of conditions. For global first-movers, there are unique advantages and disadvantages (see Chen and Pereira 1999), and on the Web, the first-mover advantage is increasingly difficult to achieve given the likelihood of "fast-followers" (from across the globe) emerging rapidly to compete for the same customers.

On the Web, the first-mover advantage has helped build brands such as *eBay* and *Amazon*. However, increasingly, this route to brand building is difficult because—unlike in the early days of the World Wide Web—the new environment is less conducive to first-mover advantage. The new environment of low entry barriers, coupled with a growing proliferation of competitors from across the globe, makes for a very small window of opportunity to establish first-mover advantage. In other words, in today's Web, the first-mover advantage can be easily negated before it is established because the Web allows "fast-followers" to emerge quickly behind the first-mover and compete for the same customers.

In the future, global web sites that are likely to enjoy the powerful advantages of branding will be those that are distinctively customized to their target markets. Further, given the global trends in e-commerce (see next section), we believe that for such a customization to be successful, it will have to be *culturally* based. We will show in the coming chapters that companies targeting global customers have little choice but to *culturally customize* their web sites if they are to successfully draw customers, build trust and loyalty, and make themselves invulnerable to competitive marketing actions.

The next section discusses various trends in global e-commerce, all of which point to the next imperative for web sites: cultural customization.

TRENDS IN E-COMMERCE

Today, global online trade is driven by the spread of free markets, increasing literacy and computer access in developing countries, deregulation and liberalization of industries, and the continuing trend of globalization across the world. It is expected that by the end of 2004, global e-commerce sales will reach $6.8 trillion, and by 2006, Forrester Research predicts, it will reach almost $12.8 trillion (*www.forrester.com*). In 2000, the global Internet population was 350 million; it is expected to jump to almost 941 million users by 2005 (*www.idc.com*).

The domination of the United States in the online marketplace is eroding due to changing online demographics, diffusion of Internet technology across the globe, and growth and acceptance of the Internet by consumers worldwide. By 2005, the U.S. share of online population is forecast to be 24 percent; a substantial part of the online population growth will come from Asia, Europe, and Latin America (*www.emarketer.com*). In revenue terms, U.S. dominance also continues to shrink; Forrester Research estimates that of the $6.8 trillion in global online sales in 2004, the United States will account for $3.2 trillion, and the rest will come from the Asia-Pacific region ($1.6 trillion), Europe ($1.5 trillion), and Latin America ($82 billion) (*www.forrester.com*). Moreover, projections from an Internet research firm, *www.globalreach.com*, show that in 2004 only 35 percent of the online population will belong to English-speaking nations, while approximately 65 percent of global Internet users will be non-English speakers (or those for whom English is a second language). Online consumers speaking Chinese (170 million), Japanese (88 million), Spanish (70 million), German (62 million), Korean (43), and French (41 million) dominate the linguistically diverse global online population. This growing, geographically and culturally diverse online population offers extraordinary opportunities in e-commerce revenues for businesses; in fact, U.S. companies not targeting international online consumers are only tapping 25 percent of the world's purchasing power (Lynch, Kent, and Srinivasan, 2001).

To appeal to these culturally diverse customers, web sites must be culturally customized as part of a larger effort to "brand" the web sites to the various global segments. The need to customize web sites is not without controversy. More specifically, it is part of the larger debate of standardization versus localization, initiated by Elinder in the 1960s and then again by Levitt in the 1980s. As the next section illustrates, not withstanding some views that favor standardization, there is overwhelming research support for the need for customization, including a five-nation study that we completed on perceptions of online customers with regard to both attitudes toward web sites and purchase intentions.

STANDARDIZATION VERSUS LOCALIZATION ON THE WEB

The debate over the appropriateness of standardization versus localization in international marketing continues to receive attention. The debate is complicated in the context of the World Wide Web as it is a global communication medium where technology makes mass customization or adaptation possible, while forces of global integration and the emergence of transnational web style (Sackmary and Scalia 1999) justify the use of a standardized web marketing and communication strategy.

The advocates of the standardization approach argue that as technology develops and is globally dispersed, cultural distance will be minimized, leading to convergence of national cultures into a homogenous global culture. On the other hand, there are a number of studies (including one discussed below) in support of customizing web sites to specific markets across the world. Research shows that consumers prefer to shop and interact in sites that are specially designed for them in their local language (Singh, Furrer, and Massimilaino 2004). More than 75 percent of Chinese and Korean online shoppers prefer web sites in Mandarin and Korean respectively (Ferranti 1999). Similarly, the French and Spanish have a strong preference for sites in their local languages (Lynch, Kent, and Srinivasan 2001). In general, online users feel more at ease when browsing web pages in their local languages. A survey by Forrester Research confirms that non-English-speaking users stay twice as long on localized web sites as they do on English-only web sites, and business users are three times more likely to make purchases online when addressed in their local language (www.forrester.com). Forrester Research also concludes that customer service costs drop when instructions are available in local languages. Several studies (Luna, Peracchio, and de Juan 2002; Simon 2001; Singh et al. 2004) confirm that country-specific web content enhances usability, reach, and web site interactivity, leading to more web traffic and business activity on the Web. And, as seen next, our research indicates the same: that web sites that are customized to specific countries enjoy strong advantages compared with those that are not.

Our study focused on web sites and consumers from five countries: Italy, India, the Netherlands, Spain, and Switzerland. Web sites from these countries were sampled and evaluated by respondents on a variety of criteria. The criteria measure *adaptation to countries* and are evaluated on a scale of 1 (Strongly Disagree) to 5 (Strongly Agree); the criteria focus on whether web sites reflect a specific country's culture, if it seems that web sites were specifically developed for a given country, if it makes individuals culturally-comfortable, and if the images, colors, information, and symbols used are reflective of a specific country.

The average scores (across the criteria) were calculated for each web site, and using percentiles, web sites for each country were categorized as High, Medium, or Low in adaptation. Next, respondents from Italy, India, the

Netherlands, and Spain were given questionnaires to evaluate the web sites on *attitude toward the site* and *purchase intention*. A total of 627 completed questionnaires were used in the analysis. As the results in Table 1.1 indicate, attitude toward the web site and purchase intention were strongly in favor of highly adapted web sites. (For details of the study, see Appendix 1.1.) Thus, it is evident that customizing web sites to diverse, global customers is important. If a company does *not* provide a customized web site, it is essentially expecting its potential customers from various parts of the world to *adapt to it*—rather than vice-versa. Obviously, such a strategy is fraught with risk as dissatisfied customers are unlikely to become loyal customers and are more likely to turn to competitors whose web sites are more in tune with their needs.

THE STATE OF WEB SITE CUSTOMIZATION

Today, the process of developing customized global web sites is termed *web site globalization*, which in turn includes two complementary processes: *web*

TABLE 1.1   Adaptation Levels, Attitude Toward Site and Purchase Intention

	Adaptation level of web site		
	High	Medium	Low
Italy			
Attitude toward site	3.60	3.57	3.34
Purchase intention	3.06	3.10	2.68
India			
Attitude toward site	4.26	3.74	3.04
Purchase intention	4.04	3.68	3.18
Netherlands			
Attitude toward site	3.48	2.97	2.87
Purchase intention	2.34	1.91	2.19
Switzerland			
Attitude toward site	3.59	3.16	2.69
Purchase intention	3.16	2.93	2.64
Spain			
Attitude toward site	4.31	3.50	2.82
Purchase intention	4.14	3.30	2.67

Note: *Attitude toward site* and *Purchase intention* measured on 1–5 scale; mean values reported in table (see details in Appendix 1.1).

Singh N., Furrer O., and Massimilaino O. (2004) To Localize or to Standardize on the Web: Empirical Evidence from Italy, India, Netherlands, Switzerland, and Spain, *Multinational Business Review*, 12(1), 69–88.

site internationalization and *web site localization*. Together, they address issues that go beyond language translation and include the need to incorporate local date, time, purchase order, zip codes, currency calculators, and a plethora of icons and features to make web sites understandable and readable by international consumers. In technical terms, *web site internationalization* is the process through which back-end technologies are used to create modular, extendable, and accessible global web site templates that support front-end customization, and *web site localization* is the process of the front-end customization, whereby web sites are adapted to meet the needs of specific international target markets (Singh and Boughton 2004). As part of web site localization there have been some efforts to address cultural issues of the relevant target customers. However, our experience with these efforts is that they tend not to be based on sound theory and careful research. As such, they do not accomplish true cultural customization; more relevant, they generally do not even accomplish the fundamentals of web site internationalization and web site localization, which are needed for successful cultural customization.

Web site internationalization, according to LISA (Localization Industry Standards Organization; *www.lisa.org*) should be culturally and technically "neutral," making it amenable for localization to specific target markets. These target markets are typically countries; however, in some instances, countries may not be the best basis for localization. Sometimes it would be more appropriate to use "locales"—defined as a language-country combination, such as French-Canada, English-Canada, German-Switzerland, and French-Switzerland (Yunker 2003).

For web site globalization efforts to be successful, it is important to involve overseas subsidiaries and local partners for their local input, and the technology must be complemented with back-end processes that ensure quality, reliability, and accountability (*www.globalsight.com*). However, several companies, either in haste to globalize or due to insufficient resources, tend to ignore the important back-end processes; instead, they develop separate global templates for different countries or use machine-translated versions of the parent home page (Singh and Boughton 2004). Idiom Technologies conducted a "Global Quotient Survey," and found that 36 percent of e-business executives interviewed have done nothing to prepare their web site's back-end processes to meet the needs of international users, while an additional third have only adjusted a minority of their site capabilities (*www.idiominc.com/worldwiseinterview.asp*).

A sound web site globalization effort, comprised of internationalization and localization, is needed to ensure successful cultural customization. The web site *www.Kodak.com* is a good example of such a globalization effort; however, as the rest of the book reveals, more must be done if it is to be a culturally customized web site.

Web Site Insight: *www.Kodak.com*

Kodak is an example of a company that has used both internationalization and localization to achieve international web presence. Initially, Kodak adopted the strategy of merely translating its English web pages into different languages, but it soon realized that plain translation was not enough to target and reach out to international users. For example, Terry Lund of Kodak explains that they translated their section on "Guide to better pictures," (a popular link at *www.Kodak.com*) into German and found that even though the translation was accurate, Germans did not find it appealing and did not like the writing style (Dana Blanenhorn, www.itmanagement.earthweb.com/entdev/article. php/609301). Thus, Kodak consulted companies in web globalization business and country in question (the localization process). For example, the Kodak trademark phrase, "Share moments, share life," has been carefully phrased in different languages, as its literal translation is not always accurate. Now Kodak is well organized, and it is ranked as one of the top global web sites on the Web. Kodak also provides international consumers their respective country pages; in this regard, it has a global gateway page containing links to more than 50 different country-specific web sites. Each country-specific web site link on the global gateway page is recognizable by the country flag and also the name of the country in the local language where appropriate (Figure 1.1).

On the Kodak web site, if you click on "Change Country/Language," you will see the web page shown in Figure 1.2:

Kodak's web page for French-Canada is seen in Figure 1.3:

Kodak's web page for English-Canada is seen in Figure 1.4: Kodak is considered a good example of web site globalization; however, we believe that Kodak has to do more, in terms of cultural customization, if its web site is to thwart future competitors and build trust and loyalty among its diverse international customers.

FIGURE I.I   *www.kodak.com*

Continues

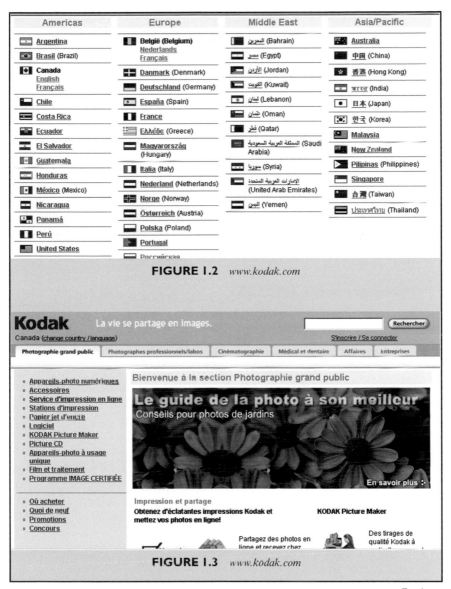

FIGURE 1.2 *www.kodak.com*

FIGURE 1.3 *www.kodak.com*

Continues

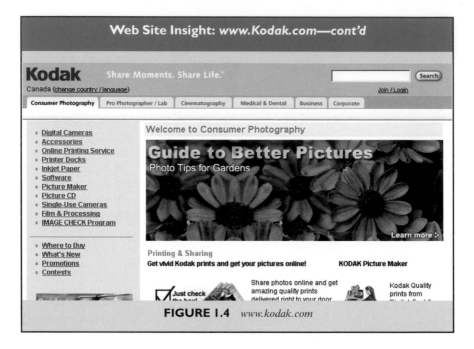

FIGURE 1.4   *www.kodak.com*

A CLASSIFICATION OF WEB SITES

To evaluate the state of web site globalization across countries and industries, we offer a classification system based on the recent literature on e-commerce globalization (Singh and Boughton 2004). Web site globalization can be studied at two levels: the back-end level and the front-end level. The back-end level involves how global templates are designed; the front-end level can be studied in terms of global or local features explicitly exhibited on the web sites. These features could be the presence or absence of a language option, machine translation versus human translation of the web pages, or display of country-specific web site options on the home page. We propose five categories of web site globalization using the front-end criteria:

1. Standardized Web Sites
2. Semi-Localized Web Sites
3. Localized Web Sites
4. Highly Localized Web Sites
5. Culturally Customized Web Sites

Standardized Web Sites

These sites have the same web content for both domestic and international users. There is no effort made to reach out to international consumers in terms of translation, internationalization, or localization.

Example: *www.Tyco.com*. Tyco International, Ltd. boasts of being a truly international company with business in over 100 countries. Tyco employs approximately 100,000 people, and its products span the fields of security and safety, medical care, plastics and adhesives, electronics, and engineered products. It offers one, standardized web site in English for all of its customers (Figures 1.5, 1.6).

FIGURE 1.5   *www.tyco.com*

FIGURE 1.6   *www.tyco.com*

Semi-Localized Web Sites

These web sites provide contact information about foreign subsidiaries; little else is offered to address the needs of their international customers.

Example: *www.Gap.com*. Founded in 1969 in San Francisco, Gap Inc. is one of the world's largest retailers and has over 4,100 stores in 3,000 locations in the United States, United Kingdom, Canada, France, Japan, and Germany. Surprisingly, this company does little to address the needs of their Japanese, French, and German online customers. It has one central U.S. web site for all of its customers, both U.S. and international customers. Gap has not been proactive in its web site globalization efforts and may find some challenges when it eventually launches international web sites. For example, if you type *www.gap.fr* you will not be directed to Gap's web site in France but to an automotive site. A Japanese customer looking for a store in say, Tokyo, will need to understand English before he can find the web page that directs customers to various country web sites, which are in English. The page that has the information on Gap stores in Tokyo is again in English (Figures 1.7, 1.8).

Localized Web Sites

These web sites offer country-specific web pages with translation, wherever relevant.

Example: *www.Dell.com*. Dell is the world's leading computer systems company. According to the company, they "design, build, and customize products and services to satisfy a range of customer requirements. From the server, storage and professional services needs of the largest global corporations to those consumers at home." The company does business directly with customers and has production facilities in North and South America, Asia,

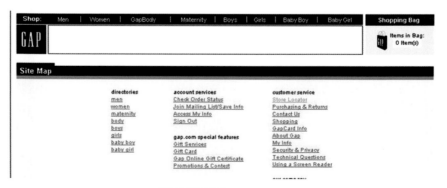

FIGURE 1.7   *www.gap.com*

FIGURE 1.8 *www.gap.com*

and Europe. Dell's web site provides country-specific web pages along with translation into the relevant language, wherever necessary (Figures 1.9, 1.10).

Highly Localized Web Sites

These web sites offer country-specific URLs with translations wherever relevant, and include relatively high levels of localization in terms of country-specific information, time, date, zip code, number formats, and so on.

Example: *www.Amazon.com.* Amazon, which started as an online bookstore, today has diversified into other areas such as apparel, music, health and beauty products, electronics and office supplies, (Figure 1.11). The company's vision is "to be earth's most customer centric company; to build a place where

FIGURE 1.9 *www.dell.com*

FIGURE 1.10 *www.dell.com*

FIGURE 1.11 *www.amazon.com*

people can come to find and discover anything they might want to buy online." The company offers unique web sites for Japan (*www.Amazon.jp*), Germany (*www.Amazon.de*), Canada (*www.Amazon.ca*), United Kingdom (*www.Amazon.co.uk*), and France (*www.Amazon.fr*) (e.g., Figure 1.12).

Culturally Customized Web Sites

These web sites exhibit designs that reflect a complete "immersion" in the culture of the target market. A comprehensive cultural customization will reflect

FIGURE 1.12   *www.amazon.jp*

three levels of cultural adaptation: perception, symbolism, and behavior (see Chapter 2 and others that follow).

Example: No web site we are aware of (see survey, next section) qualifies for this category. One web site that comes close is *www.Ikea.com*. Ikea is the low-price global furnishing giant that operates in over 30 countries. The Ikea country-language pages are a good attempt at cultural customization (Figures 1.13, 1.14). For example, their Saudi Arabia web site has the scroll-bar on the left, reflecting the *spatial orientation* element (see Chapter 2) of *perception* in Saudi culture.

WEB SITE CUSTOMIZATION: A STUDY

The classification described in the previous section was used to measure the extent of web site globalization of Forbes 900 companies. Of the 900 companies, only 598 companies were found to target international customers (Singh and Boughton, 2004). This sample comprised 307 U.S. companies, 164 European companies, and 127 companies from Asia-Pacific. Less than half of the web sites (255) fell in the "localized" and "highly localized" categories under the classification scheme, with none qualifying for the cultural customization category.

Among the 307 total U.S. web sites, 28.7 percent fell under the "highly localized" category, and 36 percent were standardized or semi-localized. A total of 13 countries in Europe were represented in the sample of 165

FIGURE 1.13 *www.ikea.com*

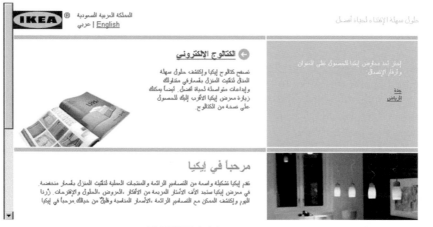

FIGURE 1.14 *www.ikea.com*

European web sites. The percentage of "highly localized" was lower than that of the United States, with 23.2 percent. The Asia-Pacific region included Australia, China, Japan, and South Korea. A total of 127 company web sites were analyzed for the Asia-Pacific region, with 19 percent qualifying to be "highly localized" and 25 percent "standardized" (see Table 1.2).

This study indicates that web site globalization has a long way to go, with almost 57 percent of company web sites categorized as *not* localized. More relevant, none of the web sites was culturally customized. At present, there is no theoretically sound framework available for web designers to approach cultural customization of web sites—a possible reason why we did not see culturally customized web sites in our study.

TABLE 1.2 State of Web Site Customization

Category	U.S. Frequency	%	Europe Frequency	%	Asia-Pacific Frequency	%	Total Frequency	%
Standardized	23	7.5	22	13.4	25	19.7	69	11.7
Semilocalized	88	28.7	39	23.8	49	38.6	176	29.4
Localized	108	35.2	65	39.6	34	26.8	207	34.6
Highly localized	88	28.7	38	23.2	19	15.0	145	24.2
Culturally Customized	0	0	0	0	0	0	0	0

Adapted from Singh and Boughton (2004).

CULTURAL CUSTOMIZATION: THE NEXT IMPERATIVE IN WEB DESIGN

Culture is often viewed as the "soft" aspect of international marketing. Its importance—thus far—is at best, seen as secondary to other elements of international marketing strategy (Mooij 2000). To this day, many international marketing managers are unclear on how to balance the cost efficiencies of standardization versus the increased costs of localization for their global products. However, there is general agreement that effective marketing entails identifying and satisfying consumer needs. Are not consumer needs a product of culture, society, and societal expectations that influence the consumer? In fact, culture prescribes broad guidelines for acceptable ways of behaving and acting in particular situations (Feather 1990), and it influences how we interact and socialize with other members of the society (Rokeach 1973) and the valences we attach to different situations (Feather 1995). It is a powerful force shaping our motivations, lifestyles, and product choices (Tse, Belk, and Zhou 1989). The advent of the Internet has created a new medium that may be especially sensitive to the values of a particular culture. The need for cultural differences to be understood by multinational corporations and the impact of culture on global business through information technology have been increasingly recognized in the information system literature. Studies have found that culturally sensitive web content enhances usability, accessibility, and web site interactivity (Fock 2000; Simon 2001). Mooij (1998) claims that advertising reflects a society's values and that effective advertising and marketing are inseparably linked to the underlying culture of the targeted group. It has been shown that advertising that reflects local cultural values is more powerful and persuasive than culturally insensitive advertising (Mueller 1987; Zandpour et al. 1994). Several researchers, therefore, have emphasized the use and appeal of country-specific cultural values when developing international advertising campaigns and communication material (Albers-Miller and Gelb 1996; Han and Shavitt 1994). It is important that marketers pay close attention to the values of a particular culture, as cultural values determine the modes of conduct and end states of existence for individuals (Pollay 1983). Given the issues discussed in this chapter, can businesses ignore culture in the context of designing web sites? The answer is a definite no, and the next chapter offers the background to understanding and implementing the cultural customization of web sites.

Visit www.theculturallycustomizedwebsite.com for additional information and updates.

CHAPTER KEYS

Given the proliferation of web sites and the growth of the Internet across the globe, it is increasingly an enormous challenge to be able to draw customers to a web site and build customer trust and loyalty.

The diversity of cultures that make up the global marketplace necessitates customizing web sites to the needs of customers from specific countries and cultures. Research studies clearly indicate that—in general—customers are more comfortable with, and also exhibit a more positive attitude toward, web sites that are consistent with their cultures and languages.

The present state of adaptation or customization of web sites is very limited—largely focused on customizing web sites in terms of language, and some superficial attributes. An important reason for this is the lack of a theoretically sound framework to guide the cultural customization of web sites.

A study of web sites using categories such as *standardized, semi-localized, localized, highly localized,* and *culturally customized* reveals that there are no truly culturally customized web sites. This suggests a tremendous opportunity for managers to move quickly and attempt cultural customization of their web sites. There is every indication that customization can help build a strong, loyal customer base. Further, it is very likely that if a company doesn't customize, it may be forced to do so in the future, driven by competitors doing the same or by increased expectations from customers.

EXERCISES

The chapter provided the frequency distribution of web sites (in terms of *standardized, semi-localized, localized, highly localized,* and *culturally customized*) for the United States, Europe, and Asia-Pacific. For example, a sample of U.S. web sites produced the following frequency distribution (Table 1.3, Figure 1.15).

TABLE 1.3   Frequency Distribution of U.S. Web Sites

Type of web site	Frequency in the U.S.
S: Standard Web Sites	23
SL: Semi-Localized Web Sites	88
L: Localized Web Sites	108
HL: Highly Localized Web Sites	88
CC: Culturally Customized Web Sites	0

Singh and Boughton (2004)

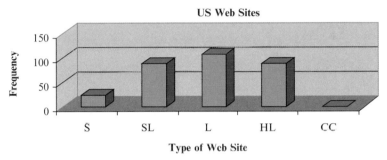

FIGURE 1.15   Frequency Distribution of U.S. Web Sites

Students

Focus on web sites of an industry of interest (e.g., a computer industry) or more broadly, on a type of business (e.g., service/industrial/consumer). Visit various company sites in that industry (or type of business) and categorize the web site as *standardized, semi-localized, localized, highly localized,* or *culturally customized* (see definitions in this chapter). Compare the frequency distribution of your web sites with that seen in Table 1.3 and Figure 1.15 for the United States in general. Are they similar or different? If different, how are they different (more standardized sites? more localized sites?)? What could be reasons for these differences?

Managers

Survey the web sites of your industry, classify them as *standardized, semi-localized, localized, highly localized,* and *culturally customized* (see definitions in this chapter.) Where does your company fall on this frequency distribution? Are you satisfied with your position? (Where do the web sites of significant other companies, such as the largest market shareholder, fall on this distribution?) If you are satisfied (e.g., you are among the few highly localized web sites in your industry), do the following: Choose another industry—ideally one that is more mature and developed than yours—that has the same/similar target market as yours. For example, the soda industry and the bottled water industry have largely overlapping target markets; so do the insurance industry and the banking industry. Survey the web sites of this *other* industry; attempt to benchmark your web site against the best site in the *other* industry. The reasoning: Customers who visit your web site also visit the web sites of the *other* industry (as both industries target the same customers); as such, even if your web site is exceptional when compared with the web sites of your industry, it may be poor compared with the web sites of the other industry.

APPENDIX 1.1

Detailed results of the study discussed on pages 5-6 are presented below.

TABLE 1.4   MANOVA Results and Post Hoc Group Comparisons

Measures	Adaptation level[a]			Tukey or Dunnet C tests[b]	
	High	Medium	Low	F	Group comparisons[c]
Italy					
Attitude toward site	3.60	3.57	3.34	2.80[*]	
Purchase intention	3.06	3.10	2.68	6.76[**]	L<M; L<H
India					
Attitude toward site	4.26	3.74	3.04	60.7[**]	L<M<H
Purchase intention	4.04	3.68	3.18	36.8[**]	L<M<H
Netherlands					
Attitude toward site	3.48	2.97	2.87	8.26[**]	L<M<H
Purchase intention	2.34	1.91	2.19	ns	
Switzerland					
Attitude toward site	3.59	3.16	2.69	19.6[**]	L<M; L<H
Purchase intention	3.16	2.93	2.64	3.4[*]	
Spain					
Attitude toward site	4.31	3.50	2.82	34.9[**]	L<M<H
Purchase intention	4.14	3.30	2.67	31.7[**]	L<M<H

[a]Mean values are reported; [*] $p < .05$; [**]$p < .01$
[b]Comparisons that are significant at $<.05$ level are reported.
[c]H = High adaptation, M = Medium adaptation, L = Low adaptation.
   Singh N., Furrer O., and Massimilaino O. (2004) To Localize or to Standardize on the Web: Empirical Evidence from Italy, India, Netherlands, Switzerland, and Spain, *Multinational Business Review*, 12(1), 69–88.

TABLE 1.5   Reliabilities (Cronbach Alphas) of Measures

Measures	Italy	India	Netherlands	Switzerland	Spain
Attitude toward site	.70	.87	.76	.79	.92
Purchase intention	.82	.78	.96	.94	.92
Cultural adaptation	.90	.60	.84	.88	.90

The results in general show that web sites depicting high levels of cultural adaptation were ranked higher, followed by medium and low adapted web sites. To further check the degree of significant differences in perception of web site effectiveness by level of adaptation, we performed a post hoc analysis. Before the post hoc analysis, we checked for homogeneity of variance, and wherever the assumption was violated, we used Dunnet's C test; otherwise, we used the Tukey (hsd) test (Morgan and Griego 1998). The post hoc analysis reveals that Indian and Spanish consumers ranked highly adapted web sites higher than medium and low adapted web sites on both *attitude toward the site* and *purchase intention*. Dutch and Swiss consumers ranked highly adapted web sites higher than low and medium adapted web sites on *attitude toward the site*, but on *purchase intention*, differences are not significant. (However, the mean values of local web sites are higher than those of other web sites.) Finally, Italian consumers only showed better *attitude toward the site* and high *purchase intention* for highly adapted web sites.

Reliability of Measures Used in Study

Besides the 4-item measure of cultural adaptation (see page 000), the other measures used in the study, Attitude toward Site and Purchase Intention, are also multi-item measures. The reliabilities of these measures in the form of Cronbach Alphas are provided in Table 1.5.

REFERENCES

Albers-Miller, N.D. and Gelb, B.D. (1996) Business Advertising Appeals as Mirror of Cultural Dimensions: A Study of Eleven Countries, *Journal of Advertising*, 25(Winter), 57–70.

Chen, H. and Pereira, A. (1999) Product Entry in International Markets: The Effect of Country-of-Origin on First-Mover Advantage, *Journal of Product and Brand Management*, Vol.8, No.3, 218–231.

Feather, N. (1990) "Bridging the Gap between Values and Action. In E. Higgins and R. Sorrentino (eds.), *Handbook of Motivation and Cognition*, Vol. 12, New York: Guilford.

Feather, N. (1995) Values, Valences, and Choice, *Journal of Personality and Social Psychology*, 68, 1135–1151.

Ferranti, M. (1999) From Global to Local, *Infoworld*, 21(41), 36–37.

Fock, H. (2000) Cultural Influences on Marketing Communication on the World Wide Web, *Paper Presented at the Multicultural Marketing Conference*, Hong Kong, Sept.

Han, S.-P. and Shavitt, S. (1994) Persuasion and Culture: Advertising Appeals in Individualistic and Collectivistic Societies, *Journal of Experimental Social Psychology*, 30(July), 8–18.

Keller, K.L. (1998) Strategic Brand Management New Jersey: Prentice-Hall.

Luna, D., Peracchio, L.A., and Juan, M.D. de (2002) Cross-Cultural and Cognitive Aspects of Web Site Navigation, *Journal of the Academy of Marketing Science*, 30(4), 397–410.

Lynch, P.D., Kent, R.J., and Srinivasan, S.S. (2001) The Global Internet Shopper: Evidence from Shopping Tasks in Twelve Countries, *Journal of Advertising Research*, 41(3), 15–23. Mooij M. de (1998) *Global Marketing and Advertising: Understanding Cultural Paradoxes*. Thousand Oaks, CA: Sage Publications.

Mooij, M. de (2000) The Future is Predictable for International Marketers, *International Marketing Review*, 17(2), 103–113.

Morgan, G.A. and Griego, O.V. (1998) *Easy Use and Interpretation of SPSS for Windows*. Mahwah, NJ: Lawrence Erlbaum Associates.

Mueller, B. (1987) Reflections of Culture: An Analysis of Japanese and American Advertising Appeals, *Journal of Advertising Research*, 27(3), 51–59.

Pollay, R.W. (1983) Measuring the Cultural Values Manifest in Advertising. In J.H. Leigh and C.R. Martin (eds.), *Current Issues and Research in Advertising*, 72–92. Ann Arbor: University of Michigan Press.

Rokeach, M. (1973) *The Nature of Human Values*. New York: Free Press.

Sackmary, B. and Scalia, L.M. (1999), Cultural Patterns of World Wide Web Business Sites: A Comparison of Mexican and U.S Companies *Paper Presented at Seventh Cross-Cultural Consumer and Business Studies Research Conference*, Cancun, Mexico.

Simon, S.J. (2001) The Impact of Culture and Gender on Web Sites: An Empirical Study, *Database for Advances in Information Systems*, 32(1), 18–37.

Singh, N. and Boughton, P.D. (2004) Measuring Web Site Globalization: A Cross-Sectional Country and Industry Level Analysis, *Journal of Web Site Promotion* (in press). *http://www.haworthpressinc.com*

Singh, N., Furrer, O., and Massimilaino, O. (2004) To Localize or to Standardize on the Web: Empirical Evidence from Italy, India, Netherlands, Switzerland, and Spain, *Multinational Business Review*, 12(1), 69–88.

Sonderegger P., Manny H., Tony J., and Gardiner K (2001) The Global User Experience, A Report from Forrester Research-*www.forrester.com*

Tellis, G., Golder, P., and Christensen, C. (2001) *Will and Vision: How Latecomers Grow to Dominate Markets*. New York: McGraw-Hill.

Thomas B. (2001) Global Trends: The Shift away from North America Gains Momentum, A Report from Forrester Research-*www.forrester.com*

Tse, D.K., Belk, R.W. and Zhou, N. (1989), "Becoming a Consumer Society: A Longitudinal and Cross-cultural Content Analysis of Print Ads from Hong Kong, The People's republic of China, and Taiwan," *Journal of Consumer Research*, 15, 457–472

Yunker, J. (2003) Beyond Borders: *Web Globalization Strategies*. Indianapolis, IN: New Riders.

Zandpour, F., and (A Team of 10 Researchers) (1994) Global Reach and Local Touch: Achieving Cultural Fitness in TV Advertising, *Journal of Advertising Research*, 34(5), 35–63.

2

THE RATIONALE FOR CULTURAL CUSTOMIZATION

This chapter lays the foundation for cultural customization of web sites and introduces three important aspects of culture: perception, symbolism, *and* behavior. *An overview of issues related to* perception *and* symbolism *is offered, highlighting their relevance in the cultural customization of web sites. The issue of cultural* behavior *is introduced in this chapter and will be dealt with in-depth in the later chapters.*

CHAPTER HIGHLIGHTS

WEB ROI

WHAT IS CULTURE?

PERCEPTION AND CULTURE

PERCEPTION: IMPLICATIONS FOR WEB SITES

SYMBOLISM AND CULTURE

SYMBOLISM: IMPLICATIONS FOR WEB SITES

BEHAVIOR AND CULTURE

WEB ROI

According to Bryan Eisenberg of *www.clickz.com*, the Web has evolved over four phases: *the technology phase* (a focus on gopher and bulletin boards), *the design phase* (a focus on designing attractive sites), *the marketing phase* (a time of unfettered marketing spending with little concern for revenues and profits, leading to the technology bubble), and today, *the business phase*, with a focus on Web ROI—return on *web* investment.

In the context of web ROI, the key issue is *conversion rate*, a measure of a web site's ability to persuade visitors to take the action that it wants them to take (e.g., make a purchase). Conversion is the first step to building loyalty, trust, and repeat purchase behavior.

If you are a global marketer, the visitors, who must be "persuaded" to take the action you want them to take, are typically drawn from various cultures. The challenge of persuading them is inextricably linked to their respective cultures because culture impacts how we perceive, process, and interpret information (Kale 1991; Triandis 1982). Consumers decipher the meanings in the world around them through a systematic mental process that processes, sorts, and interprets every bit of information. This mental process, or as Hofstede (1980) calls it, "software of the mind," is called culture, which is comprised of group-related perceptions, attitudes, values, and belief systems (Singer 1998). This cultural effect is so powerful, that Hall (1976) says that people *cannot* act or interact in any meaningful way except through the medium of culture.

Various studies have shown the impact of culture on consumer behavior and how it shapes our motivations. Cross-cultural differences in color preferences, self-perception, field dependence, sex role portrayal, and advertising content have been reported by several previous studies. Recent research by various consultancy firms and organizations (e.g., Forrester Research, Uniscape, LISA) and academics (Fock 2000; Lynch, Kent, and Srinivasan 2001; Simon 2001) indicate differences in beliefs, perceptions, and buying behavior among global Internet users. There is good reason for these differences; Singh, Furrer, and Massimilaino (2004) show that the Web is inherently an interactive com-

TABLE 2.1   The Web: A Cultural Document

Web characteristic	Cultural implication
The Web is an open network with global access.	The Web is viewed by people across countries and cultures, thus lending itself to vast cultural variability.
The inherent interactive nature of the Web.	A medium that lends itself to culturally sensitive dialogue.
The Web is characterized by hyperlinks and self-search options.	Hyperlinks and self-search options rely on consumer motivation to browse; therefore, if web content is not customized for global customers on an individual basis, the interactive efforts might be wasted (Fock 2000).
Web technologies can help capture customer data that can be used for customization.	Using customer databases and software, country-specific and culture-specific profiles can be created and used to better meet diverse customer needs.
Media convergence and broadband technology make the Web an ideal medium to interact with audio, video, graphics, and text.	Media convergence on the Web can be used to develop culture-specific themes, pictures, videos, and sounds.
On the Web, the capacity to hold visitors' attention, the "flow state," is an important challenge.	The web sites that are culturally congruent are more likely to engage the users (Simon 2001).

Adapted from: Singh N., Zhao H., and Hu X. (2004).

munication medium, and as such, a cultural document (see Table 2.1). The issue of "flow state" listed as a Web characteristic in Table 2.1 is an important one because online consumers must enjoy the experience or "flow" during a visit to a web site; this is achieved when a sufficiently motivated user perceives a balance between his or her skills and challenges of the interaction, together with focused attention (Csikszentmihalyi and LeFevre 1989). This optimal experience or "flow" formalizes and extends a sense of playfulness; thus, people find the interactive experience cognitively enjoyable (Csikszentmihalyi 2000). However, when confronted with a different language (or second language), foreign signs and symbols, and non-local web content that is culturally incongruent, there is more stress on an individual, leading to diminished control over the interaction and loss of focus (Luna, Peracchio, and de Juan 2002). For example, Simon (1999) reports that Westerners want navigation aids that make browsing easier, while Asians and Latin Americans seek aids that can change the appearance of the web site and use of animated tools.

According to Luna, Peracchio, and de Juan (2002), culturally congruent web content decreases cognitive effort to process information on the site and represents an environment where demands are clearer, leading to easier navigation and favorable attitude toward the web site. This is because categorizing, processing, and interpreting culturally congruent communication is facilitated by cultural schemas that store information in simple, broad, and culturally consistent categories (D'Andrade 1992). Schemas are simple elements or conceptual structures, which serve as prototypes for underlying real world experiences (Casson 1983; D'Andrade 1992; Quinn and Holland 1987; see Singh 2004 for extended discussion on schemas and cultural models). The cultural schemas we develop are a result of adaptation to the environment we live in and the way we have been taught to see things in our culture. As such, web users from different countries tend to prefer different web site characteristics depending on their distinct needs in terms of navigation, security, product information, customer service, shopping tools, and other features (Fink and Laupase 2000; Luna, Peracchio, and de Juan 2002; Simon 1999, 2001). Thus, in a world where customers are one click away from a competitor's web site, and the number of competitors keeps multiplying, companies need every edge possible to maximize conversion rates, customer trust, loyalty, and ultimately, long-term return on Web investment. In this context, it would be disastrous to overlook what has been established as a key element in affecting consumer preferences: culture.

Global Brands and Diverse Customers

Some managers are of the opinion that the power of their global brands is such that they transcend cultural differences among global consumers. In other words, they are of the view that global brands *need not* customize their web sites to specific countries or cultures because the brand equity is so strong that a standardized web site will suffice to

Continues

Global Brands and Diverse Customers—cont'd

support its global customers. Or, managers feel that they *should not* customize because any customization effort detracts from the standard, uniform identity of the brand and may actually affect it adversely.

Our research (see study below) indicates that this is not likely to be a sound business strategy, at least not in the case of web sites; results of our study indicate customers feel empowered and are more comfortable with even small levels of customization, let alone comprehensive cultural customization.

Examples of global brands that continue to offer a standardized web site for all their culturally diverse customers all over the world are *Gap, Inc.*, the American retail powerhouse (see Chapter 1 for details of its site) and *Marks and Spencer*, the British retailing giant.

Marks and Spencer has one, standardized web site (as of July 2004, *www.marksandspencer.com*; see Figures 2.1, 2.2), although it has 541 stores in 30 countries and uses the slogan, "Marks and Spencer is trusted and loved the world over." Moreover, this retailer boasts of a variety of awards including the following:

World's Leading Retailer 2004 (Dow Jones Sustainability Index)
High Street Retailer of the Year 2003 (Prima Magazine)
Highest Ranked UK Company; Highest Ranked Retailer in the World (Financial Times)
The Queen's Award for Enterprise Innovation

If a customer in Hong Kong wants to access Marks and Spencer, he or she is forced to log onto the British web site and then click through a couple of screens to "find a local store" near him or her. However successful Marks and Spencer is at present, we believe that it is losing an opportunity to be even more successful by customizing their web site to their diverse customer segments.

The Study

We studied online customers (Singh, Furrer, and Massimilaino 2004) from Italy, India, the Netherlands, Spain, and Switzerland, in an attempt to address the following: do online customers view the brand's "home" web site more favorably than a culturally customized web site? Since there are few culturally customized web sites to make a valid sample, we did the next best thing: we sampled (1) Standard Web Sites (the "home" sites of U.S. multinationals (e.g., *www.Dell.com*), (2) Adapted Web Sites (web sites of multinational American companies that have been specifically designed for the given country (e.g., Dell's Italian web site *www.dell.it*), and (3) Local Web Sites (a domestic web site in the given country, from the same the industry (e.g., Local Italian company: *www.chl.it*). In more detail, a requirement for including a company's web site as a Standard Web Site was that the company had separate web sites targeting other countries; criteria for Adapted Web Sites included country-specific global web templates reflected in the country-specific URLs like .it (Italy), .in (India), .nl (the Netherlands), .es (Spain), and .ch (Switzerland), and a degree of localization in the form of country-specific language, time, date, zip code, currency, and number formats. To qualify as a Local Web Site, the site had to belong to a domestic company in the same industry, targeting to the local consumers of that country.

Each of the Italian, Spanish, Indian, Swiss, and Dutch respondents visited their respective sites (Standard, Adapted, and Local) and was asked to complete a questionnaire about their *attitude toward site* and their *purchase intention*, on a scale of 1-5 (Table 2.2). The results indicate that, in general (except for in the Netherlands), customers have a more favorable attitude to Local Web Sites than to Adapted or Standardized Web Sites. This suggests that brands such as the Gap and Marks and Spencer, which offer a standardized, one-size-fits-all web site to cater to the needs of the global market, may not be following a sound strategy. More specifically, even if the Gap and Marks and Spencer are seemingly successful with their present web strategy, we contend that they can be even more successful with an "adapted" strategy (or, as the rest of the book will suggest, a culturally customized strategy). More importantly, a culturally customized web site will help build customer loyalty—the best defense against competitors—both present and those looming in the future.

FIGURE 2.1   *www.marksandspencer.com*

FIGURE 2.2   *www.marksandspencer.com*

Continues

Global Brands and Diverse Customers—cont'd

TABLE 2.2   Type of Web Site, Attitude toward Site, and Purchase Intention

	Local	Adapted	Standard
Italy			
Attitude toward site	3.72	3.41	3.38
Purchase intention	3.17	2.89	2.82
India			
Attitude toward site	3.90	3.85	3.27
Purchase intention	3.90	3.64	3.35
Netherlands			
Attitude toward site	3.16	2.94	3.16
Purchase intention	2.06	2.18	2.13
Switzerland			
Attitude toward site	2.98	3.15	3.06
Purchase intention	3.08	2.91	2.64
Spain			
Attitude toward site	4.04	3.46	3.01
Purchase intention	3.89	3.30	2.81

Note: Mean values are reported. For details of the statistical analysis, see Appendix 2.1. Singh et al (2004).

WHAT IS CULTURE?

Culture has attracted the attention of scholars for over a century; researchers studying culture have spanned the fields of anthropology, psychology, and international business. Although various definitions of culture have been proposed over the years, there has been an increasing acceptance that the theme of "shared values" is central to any definition of culture. Among the first scholars to focus on shared values were Kroeber and Kluckhohn (1952), and their definition of culture is often referred to by academic scholars:

> Culture consists in *patterned* ways of thinking, feeling and reacting, acquired and transmitted mainly by symbols, constituting the distinctive achievements of human groups, including their embodiment in artifacts; the essential core of culture consists of traditional (i.e., historically derived and selected) ideas and especially their *attached values*. (Kroeber A.L. and Kluckhohn F., p. 181; emphasis added)

This definition has influenced subsequent scholars who have continued to use the themes of *patterned thinking* and *shared values* in defining culture (Geertz 1973; Hofstede, 1980; Triandis 1972). An obvious question that arises in the context of *shared values* is the definition of "value." Again, we have various definitions for value; one popular definition is by Rokeach (1979): "a value system is an enduring organization of beliefs concerning preferable modes of conduct" (5).

Further, common to all definitions of culture is the explicit or implicit recognition of three key factors: *perception, symbolism,* and *behavior.* Together, they help establish *patterned thinking* and a *shared value* system. This chapter provides a brief overview of issues regarding perception and symbolism, introduces the relevance of cultural behavior, and attempts to tie them to issues in web site design.

PERCEPTION AND CULTURE

Perception is the process by which individuals select, filter, organize, and interpret information to create a meaningful picture of the world.

Perception and Culture: An Example

A group of senior citizens from the United States and India were asked to visualize the following statement: *A lady dressed in white, in a place of worship.* A majority of the Americans visualized *a bride at an altar.* A majority of the Indians visualized *a widow in prayer.* In most Western countries, brides dress in white; in India and many parts of Asia, brides traditionally do not wear white, but widows do. Although these trends are changing, it would be consistent with the culture and perception of the older generations in both India and the United States.

More specifically, perception envelops a broad area of human processes ranging from sensation to concept formation (Segal et al. 1966). A key aspect of perception is the filtering and processing of environmental stimuli. At the filtering and processing stages, cultural differences interact with the environment to play an important role in processing information (Berry et al. 1992). The impact of culture on perception can be traced to the works of Rivers, Sapir, and Whorf in the early 1900s. Works by Segal, Campbell, and Herskovits (1966), Deregowski (1980), and Detweiler (1978) lend further support to the thesis that culture impacts perception. Of specific interest to web design are the effects of *environment, language,* and *color* on perception.

Perception and Environment

Cognitive psychologists believe that perception is impacted by emotions, motivations, expectations—and the *physical environment.* To the extent that different cultures live in different physical environments, perception is affected. The "carpentered world" hypothesis postulates that people living in environments shaped by urban living interpret non-rectangular figures as representations of rectangular figures (Berry et al. 1992). In the Western world, people are generally exposed to a physical environment of straight lines and right angles (rooms, houses, buildings, roads, railway lines, etc.). Such an environment is rich in perspective cues to distance. This may not be the case in many other parts of the world, producing differences in perception of shapes and images, leading to the carpentered world hypothesis.

The Carpentered-World Hypothesis

Most people in the Western world live in a "carpentered world"—filled with straight lines, angles, and cuboids. This cultural background will tend to produce the Muller-Lyer illusion, whereby individuals perceive two lines to be of different lengths (see Figure 2.3A) even though both lines are of the same length. It would also cause such individuals to view the two figures as a single three-dimensional object.

Research in the 1960s revealed Africans and Phillipinos didn't experience the illusion as Europeans and Americans did. For example, the African Zulus have a "circular culture"; —they live in round huts, plough their fields in curves, and most of their possessions are rounded or circular in shape. In other words, the Muller-Lyer illusion is experienced by people in the West because they interpret the shape based on their experience with their daily physical environment—leading them to add a third dimension of depth that doesn't actually exist in the diagram.

Similarly, most people in the West will see Figure 2.3B as three-dimensional and Figure 2.3C as two-dimensional, even though they are the same figure. Studies have shown that many other cultures perceive both as two-dimensional.

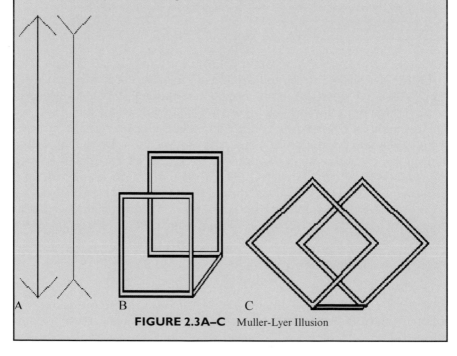

FIGURE 2.3A–C   Muller-Lyer Illusion

Perception and Language

Linguistic theory offers various views on the effect of language on thought and, thus, perception. A widely discussed view in this area is that of Edward Sapir and his student, Benjamin Lee Whorf. A commonly quoted passage representing this view is the following:

> Human beings do not live in the objective world alone, nor alone in the world of social activity as ordinarily understood, but are very much at the mercy of the particular language which has become the medium of expression for their society. It is quite an illusion to imagine that one adjusts to reality essentially without the use of language and that language is merely an incidental means of solving specific problems of communication or reflection. The fact of the matter is that the "real world" is to a large extent unconsciously built upon the language habits of the group. No two languages are ever sufficiently similar to be considered as representing the same social reality. The worlds in which different societies live are distinct worlds, not merely the same world with different labels attached. (Sapir 1958/1929, 67)

Sapir's views are reflected in the Sapir-Whorf hypothesis; it proposes that language provides conceptual categories that influence how people encode and store knowledge. As such, to the extent that languages vary across the globe, individuals—and consumers—vary in their methods of coding and storing information.

Sapir-Whorf Hypothesis

The Sapir-Whorf hypothesis claims that in our attempt to understand our world, we force structure on it—and the way we do it is using our language. The so-called strong version of the hypothesis—considered controversial—states that language *decides* our thoughts and experiences as well as helping us express them. The weaker and less controversial form states that language *shapes* our understanding of the world. For example, the language of the Hopi Indians does not have a word for "time"; as such, their understanding of the world is different from those languages that express time; the Balinese have a spatially different orientation, based on an absolute reference system of geographic points in the language (Wassman and Dasen 1998). Even simple facts are used to explain the relevance of the hypothesis. For example, the English language has one word for "corner," whereas in Spanish there are multiple words for the same, including "inside corner" and "outside corner." Russian, Spanish, and Italian have no direct translation for "blue."

The Sapir-Whorf hypothesis is controversial; however, it has not been effectively disputed or completely defended, and so it continues to receive research interest.

There is substantial research on the effect of language on how people think; for example, it was found that Chinese learn faster with visual inputs because of the pictographic nature of Chinese script (Turnage and McGinnies 1973). Kaplan (1966) observed that English writing is correlated to linear thinking, Semitic writing facilitates parallel thinking, and South and East Asia writing is characterized by non-linear thinking.

Thus, language provides the fundamental categories or set of forms that serve as code for other complex cultural forms (Goodenough 1981), and in doing so, language creates a unique cognitive-cultural system through which people categorize, process, and interpret environmental stimuli.

Perception and Color

Research has shown that language influences our perception of color, as well as our cognitive organization of color. People of different cultures do not perceive colors the same way. Different cultures may use different terms for colors; most interesting, they may assign names to unusual parts of the color spectrum. In other words, not all cultures "slice" the color spectrum the same way. Different cultures divide the rainbow in various ways; as such, VIB-GYOR (Violet, Indigo, Blue, Green, Yellow, Orange, Red) is culturally arbitrary (Segal et al. 1966) to the Western world. In this context, provocative questions that challenge researchers include: Are we able to see or distinguish only those colors that our languages have taught us? Does our color perception change when we learn a new language?

Color and Culture

Various cultures slice the color spectrum in different ways. The Japanese identify the color aoi—a color that is not easily translated in English. The best we can say is that green is a shade of aoi, or that aoi is a shade of green. The Zuni Indians have the same word for yellow and orange. The Ibibio people of Nigeria recognize only four colors (*www.putlearningfirst.com*).

According to the study by Berlin and Kay (1969), cultures and their languages use colors in a systematic way: black and white are the most readily distinguished colors across cultures; the third is red, followed by either green and yellow or yellow and green; the sixth is blue, and the seventh is brown. They are followed by orange, pink, purple, and brown. Together these form the 11 basic colors. A key conclusion of Berlin and Kay's work is the following: if a primitive language has only two basic colors, it is always black and white; for languages with only three basic colors, it is black, white, and red, and so on.

PERCEPTION: IMPLICATIONS FOR WEB SITES

When designing web sites, the previously discussed perceptual effects of the *environment*, *language*, and *color* can have profound influence on the appeal, usability, and performance of the web site. They influence the spatial orientation of the content, text length, navigational modes, translation equivalence, language dialects, and color categories (Singh 2003).

Spatial Orientation

By spatial orientation, we mean how the web content is structured. According to Barber and Badre (1998), spatial orientation has a direct effect on web site usability because it affects visual perception. For example, many of the oriental scripts (Japanese, Korean, Chinese) are justified and read vertically; on the other hand, Arabic is read from right to left, and English is read left to right. Thus, for Arabic readers, a left-justified web page might not be visually appealing. Examples of Arabic and Chinese web sites can be seen in Figures 2.4 and 2.5. Figure 2.4 is a web page from *www.arabia.com*, where the layout flows from right to left. Figure 2.5 is the web site of Nankai University, a Chinese university (*www.nankai.edu.cn*).

Attention also needs to be paid on how graphics and composition is structured on the web page. For example, in Western cultures central composition is relatively uncommon, but in oriental cultures centering is not only preferred but is also a norm when depicting visual art and graphics (Mooij 2004).

Navigation Modes

The variations in language readability (left to right, or right to left, or vertical) across cultures also impact how people browse web pages. For example, studies by researchers such as Barber and Badre (1998) show that people in Arabic cultures who are used to reading from right to left prefer navigation bars in a similar

FIGURE 2.4 *www.arabia.com*

FIGURE 2.5   *www.nankai.edu.cn*

sequence (as opposed to the scroll bar on the right-hand side, which is the norm for Western audiences). For example, the Swedish retailing company Ikea has taken note of this cultural preference, as seen in its Kuwait web site (Figure 2.6).

Translation Equivalence

When translating web sites, special attention is needed on how various concepts, words, and sentences are translated from one language to another.

FIGURE 2.6   *www.ikea.com*

Multilingual software packages that are in vogue today are susceptible to various translation errors in the form of *idiomatic equivalence, vocabulary equivalence,* and *conceptual equivalence.* Other factors that impact translation equivalence include *dialects, text length,* and *color categories.*

Idiomatic Equivalence

Each language has its unique idioms, and it is often challenging to translate them appropriately. For example, how does one translate American idioms such as *cross your fingers* or *fighting tooth and nail?*

Translation: Idiomatic Equivalence

Each language has its own unique idioms that may be difficult or impossible to translate exactly. For example, translating the following idioms commonly used in American English might be challenging in another language:

Chip off the old block
Barking up the wrong tree
Feeling blue
Out on the town
An axe to grind
The writing on the wall
Under the gun
At the drop of a hat
Down to the wire
Beating around the bush

Vocabulary Equivalence

How does one translate when a word has many meanings in one language, or when it has no equivalent? For example, Shenkar and von Glinow (1994) note that a word such as autonomy cannot be adequately translated into Chinese, and that alternate Chinese terms, such as *zi zhu quan* "right of self-determination," convey a quite different meaning.

Translation: Vocabulary Equivalence

A language may not have words that convey the exact or equivalent meaning for translation, as the following three examples illustrate.

(1) As an example, Levine (1988) talks about the challenges of translating into Portuguese a questionnaire containing the English verb "to wait":

Continues

Translation: Vocabulary Equivalence—cont'd

Several of our questions were concerned with how long the respondent would wait for someone *to arrive* versus *when they hoped the person would arrive* versus *when they actually expected the person would come*. Unfortunately for us, it turns out that the terms *to wait, to hope* and *to expect* are all typically translated as the single verb *esperar* in Portuguese. (pp. 48–49)

Expanding on the previous example regarding translating various types of "waiting," Usunier (1999) says:

There is a sort of continuum across languages in the accuracy of description of the waiting phenomenon. The French language, which lies somewhere between English and Portuguese in terms of temporal accuracy, uses two words: *attendre* (to wait) and *espérer* (to hope). *To expect* has no direct equivalent in French and must be translated by a lengthy circumlocution, *compter sur l'arrivée de.*

(2) Another example of vocabulary equivalence (or the lack of it) is the Japanese response to the Potsdam Declaration in July 1945, leading to the bombing of Hiroshima and Nagasaki. The Allies, armed with the atom bomb, issued the Potsdam Declaration, offering an ultimatum to Japan: surrender unconditionally or face the consequences. Historians say that the Japanese clearly understood the implications of the atom bomb being used on them; their dilemma was to find a more face-saving option than unconditional surrender. The Japanese Premier Kantaro Suzuko announced that the Cabinet had taken a stance of *mokusatsu*, which has no exact meaning in English and can be translated as "making no comment" or "ignoring." The Japanese Cabinet intended the former meaning, and not the latter, as they wanted more time to discuss and decide their response (including the possibility of getting Russia involved to broker a surrender.) Instead, it was translated in the Allied world as the Japanese "ignoring" the ultimatum (some say it was translated as "rejecting" the ultimatum), leading to the destruction of Hiroshima and Nagasaki.

(3) Yet another example is the word corner in English, which has multiple translations in Spanish. For example, as a noun, "corner" has the following seven different translations in Spanish (Collins Concise Spanish Dictionary 2002.)

```
CORNER (Noun) (< angle)
[of object] (outer) ángulo m; esquina f
(inner) rincón m
[of mouth] comisura f
[of eye] rabillo m
(< bend in road) curva f; recodo m
```

If we look beyond the noun form of corner (e.g., transitive verb, intransitive verb, etc.), there are even more translations in Spanish. Complicating matters further is the fact that there is no "universal Spanish." For example, there are substantial differences in the Spanish spoken in Argentina, Colombia, and Mexico. The English word "assembly" translates as "equippo" in Argentina, "ensamblaje" in Colombia, and "montaje" in Mexico (Yunker 2003).

Conceptual Equivalence

How does one translate to ensure that exact conceptual meaning is retained in translation? As we saw, the Japanese word *mokusatsu* has more than one meaning, and unless one has a conceptual understanding of its use, errors will result (as seen on the previous page).

Translation: Conceptual Equivalence

Usunier (1999) says,

By looking at how trust is expressed in four languages (English, French, German, and Japanese), we can derive some insights on which aspects of the concept are put in the forefront by the corresponding cultures. The English concept of Trust is the reliance on and confidence in the truth, worth, reliability of a person or thing. Reliance is central in the Anglo-Saxon concept of trust, that is why the legal institution of trust has been highly developed in the Common law tradition whereas it is nonexistent in the Roman-Germanic tradition. The German concept is based on two verbs: *trauen* and *vertrauen*, both of them meaning literally to "trust". However, Germans use the first form, *trauen*, mostly in the negative sense, "Ich traue Dir nicht" ("I do not trust you"), and the second in the positive sense "Ich vertraue Dir" ("I trust you"). The prefix *Ver* indicates a transformation; this documents the worldview which lies behind the German concept of trust: (1) the initial position is distrust (2) only after a favourable change has occurred can trust be established. The German *Vertrauen* evokes the process of changing an initial trustless situation into one in which the parties have built confidence into the relationship.

The French notion of *confiance*, similarly as in other Romance languages, is based on the Latin confidentia, a compound of cum (with, shared) and fides (faith, belief): the notion of sharing common beliefs, religion or group membership, is central to the Latin concept of trust. *Confiance* assumes similarity as a pre-requisite for a trustful relationship. There is only one word in French for "trust" and "confidence" suggesting the relative unsophistication of the French low-trust culture in comparison to English and German languages. Luhmann (1988), a German writing in English, makes a sharp distinction between "confidence," that is, a broad feeling that our expectations will not be disappointed, and "trust" which requires engagement of the self and rational evaluations of risks, a difference which does not exist in French. Finally, the Japanese word for trust is *shin-yô* meaning literally: sincere business; it is based on a compound of *shin*, a character for "sincerity" and *yô* which means literally "something to do, a business," (Sakade, 1982). The Japanese *shin-yô* insists on the orientation of trust towards the future, a common enterprise and the sincere expectations of the parties." (Usunier, 1999)

The popular business press has described many a blunder due to lack of translation equivalence. For example, the Coors slogan, "turn it loose" became "suffer from diarrhea" in Spanish; Kentucky Fried Chicken's "finger licking good" translated into Chinese as "eat your fingers off"; Clairol's Curling Iron, "Mist Stick" didn't translate well in Germany given that mist in German means "manure" (Yunker 2003). The Web too has its share of translation or cultural blunders (e.g., as of November 2004, a bench named Fartfull is available on *www.Ikea.com*). Machine translations are particularly prone to serious errors. Take, for example, the word "home page," which to most English-speaking nations will mean the main page of the web site, but for French that same page is referred to as the "welcome page" and for the Spaniards it is referred to simply as "first page" (Radzievsky and Radzievsky 1998). Another example is the English word "sale," commonly used on web sites to show sales order or a seasonal sale or just a sale on goods or services; however, in French sale means "dirty." Thus, a culturally sensitive web site should pay close attention to not only the translation but also how information is being perceived and interpreted. One method that can help immensely in translation is to do a back translation to search for inconsistencies and errors in translation. Also, according to Rockwell (1998), special attention should be paid when translating roman-based alphabets (English, French, German) to non-roman-based alphabets (Chinese, Japanese, Korean) as the rules of bolding, underlining, capitalizing, and font selection vary between these two sets of alphabets.

Sort order is another problem encountered when translating from one language to another. For example, in Swedish some extended characters get sorted after the letter Z. Similarly, among Oriental languages characters are sorted by brush stroke order and not based on A to Z (*www.sdlintl.com*). Thus, attention should be paid when selecting character sets, character fonts, collating sequences, and sort order. Attention also needs to be paid to the layout of date, time, currency, zip code, telephone numbers, measurement units, and number formats, as they differ from country to country.

Dialects

Language not only differs among cultures but also among various subcultures in the form of different dialects. Even though the United States and Britain are considered culturally similar, English usage differs significantly between these two countries.

Translation: Dialects

Below are some examples of how English is spoken and written by Americans and the British.

(1) Different Words, Same Meaning

American	British
Truck	Lorry
Eraser	Rubber
Chips	Crisps
Fries	Chips
Hood (car)	Bonnet
Trunk (car)	Boot
Mudguard	Fender
Trash Can	Dust Bin

Cookie	Biscuit
Biscuit	Scone
Candy	Sweets
Baked Potato	Jacket Potato
Raincoat	Mac (Macintosh)
Glue	Gum

(2) Same Words, Different Spelling

American	*British*
Judgment	Judgement
Curb	Kerb
License (noun)	Licence
Maneuver	Manoeuvre
Neighbor	Neighbour
Organization	Organisation
Aging	Ageing
Pajamas	Pyjamas
Skeptical	Sceptical
Tire	Tyre
Gray	Grey
Draft	Draught

There are even more variations of English in Australia, India, Canada, South Africa and 52 nations where English is an official language. Similarly, Spanish is a language of about 19 different countries and thus has a variety of dialects ranging from Castilian to Latin American dialects.

Text Length

Text length determines the number of web pages needed for the web site for a particular target country. For example, when translating into languages that use Roman-based alphabets, the size of the text is expected to go up by 30 percent (Rockwell, 1998). Truncation occurs when word length varies between languages and the words that are longer get truncated due to limited web space. SDL, a localization company, recommends that as a general rule it is better to allow a large section of text to expand by 30 percent, while single word and terms can expand up to 400 percent (*www.sdintl.com*).

Translation: Text Length

1. If one translates the word *katarta* from Australian aboriginal language Pinupti, it would be "to the hole left by a goanna when it has broken the surface of its burrow after hibernation." Yes, it would take 17 words to translate it into English (*www.venus.va.com.au*). Even though languages like Pinupti seem to be of little relevance to the Web today, it is just a matter of time before all languages will have relevance on the Web.
2. Chinese translation typically shrinks 10% in size from English (*www.advancedlanguage.com*).

Text length should not only be carefully considered when translating text but also when dealing with graphics, especially if graphics contain embedded text. Thus, text length has implications for graphic use, font size, line length, and scan order for the page.

Color Categories

Cross-cultural differences in categorizing color and color combinations arise because the cultural vocabulary limits the color discriminations people can make. For example, as described earlier, the Japanese identify the color *aoi*, a color that is not easily translated in English. *Aoi* is best described as a shade of green or that green is a shade of *aoi*. Eskimos have a long list of words to describe snow and its colors; similarly in India, the color brown can be broken down in several categories. Indians distinguish between various shades of brown; matrimonial advertisements characterize the complexion of individuals as wheatish-brown, wheatish, wheatish-medium, wheatish-dark, tan, dark-tan, light-tan, light-almond, slightly-fair, and so on. Further, color is used to express moods and emotions. In some cultures yellow is associated with envy, and in others it is green. It is also used to express types of people, situations, and things, and generally, each language has its accepted color associations. For example, in Japanese, being stark naked is referred to as being "red naked" (*sekirara*); a perfect stranger is called a "red stranger" (*aka no tanin*), and a sincere heart is called a "red heart" (*akai kokoro*).

Translation: Languages and Color Associations

German and Black
"To drive black" (*schwarz fahren*) means to drive without a license or travel without a ticket.
A "black seer" is either a pessimist or a person who watches German TV without getting the required license.
A "black sender," however, is a private broadcasting station.
Japanese and Blue
A Caucasian foreigner is said to be a blue-eyed outsider (*aoi me no gaijin*).
A vegetable shop is called a "blue-things shop" (*aomonoya*).
Green moss is called "blue moss" (*aogoke*).
An anxious sigh is called a "blue breath" (*ao-iki*).
A brothel is called a "blue tower" (*seiryoo*).
    (Source: Professor Randy A. Oldaker, Department of Foreign Languages, West Virginia University at Parkersburg; personal communication)

SYMBOLISM AND CULTURE

Symbolism is the system of representations and symbols. According to Geertz (1973, p.89), "culture is historically transmitted pattern of meanings embodied in symbols, a system of inherited conception." Thus, symbols are the vehicles through which cultural information in the form of tacit knowledge is passed from one generation to the other.

In marketing and advertising, the study of symbols as means of understanding material culture has been gaining attention of consumer researchers. The earliest attempt was from Levy (1959) in the article, "Symbols for Sale." More recently consumer researchers like David Mick, Elizabeth Hirschman, Grant McCracken, Morris Holbrook, and Russell Belk have popularized semiotic or symbolic analysis of consumer culture. The argument presented for studying the symbols of society is that consumers behave based on the meaning they ascribe to marketplace stimuli (Mick 1986). For example, advertising is seen as a medium through which meaning constantly pours from the culturally constituted world to consumer goods (McCracken 1986). Thus signs, symbols, icons, rituals, and myths are an important part of the material culture, yet marketers have paid little attention to this tacit side of consumer knowledge. The result of not understanding the symbolic-material culture is numerous marketing blunders that marketers have committed across cultures. For example, a cosmetic company marketing in Japan used the theme of Nero coming to life when he sees a girl wearing their brand of lipstick, but the theme was not well understood in Japan, as the myth of Nero was not a part of Japanese culture (Ricks et al. 1974). Similarly, the swastika is a sacred symbol for Hindus and widely used as a product symbol in India; the same symbol would enrage most of the Western world.

Semiotics is the study of signs and symbols. According to Mick (1986), semiotic analysis includes understanding the structures of meaning producing events at both verbal and non-verbal levels. Peirce (1931–1958) has categorized signs into *icons*, *indexes*, and *symbols*. An icon bears a resemblance to its object, for example, an "X" over a figure of a cigarette is an icon for "no smoking." Index has a direct link between sign and the object it represents, for example, *smoke* is an index of *fire*. Symbols are the most subtle and powerful representations of cultural thought and acquire meaning through convention and practice.

Symbolism: Implications for Web Sites

As emphasized earlier, the Web can be considered to be a cultural document; as such it is important to be sensitive as to how signs and symbols are used in the text and graphics. Barber and Badre (1998) use the term "cultural markers" to signify interface design elements and features that would be preferred and understood by a particular cultural group. Furthermore, they emphasize that cultural markers have the potential to improve the usability of the site for individuals from that particular culture. Cultural sensitivity of the web sites can be analyzed in terms of country-specific symbols, icons, and color symbolism.

Country-Specific Symbols

Country-specific symbols include anything that portrays a way of life or culturally specific knowledge (Singh 2003). For example, in Arabic cultures pictures of women and animals are disliked and discouraged, while elaborate text in calligraphic style is acceptable and liked. Furthermore, the use of visual metaphors from religions such as the cross, the crescent, or a star, as well as animal figures, taboo words, graphics of hand gestures, aesthetic codes, and forbidden food may require detailed research in a specific country. In India the swastika as a religious symbol is extensively used, as it is seen as a sign of good luck and fertility. It is not uncommon to see the swastika on product labels, brands, packaging, web sites (see Figure 2.7) and even in advertisements in India.

www.naturalcaffeine.com

NATURAL CAFFEINE

HOME

Shri Ahimsa Mines & Minerals Ltd.

Natural
Caffeine

Company
Profile

Contact
Us

LINKS

MR. NEMI CHAND JAIN, Managing Director of the Company, is a Management Post Graduate (Master of Management Studies), from BI.T.S., PILANI,a Premier Educational Institution of India. He promoted Ahinsha Chemicals Ltd, which is a leading manufacturer of Natural Caffeine in Asia and has a well established reputation amongst the Multinational Pharmaceutical Companies as well as Soft Drink Manufacturers. With his more than 20 years experience in manufacturing Natural Caffeine, MR. NEMI CHAND JAIN Promoted this Company to set up world class **NATURALCAFFEINE** Manufacturing facility to meet the growing demand of Natural caffeine. Our Product meets the stringent specification of soft drink manufacturers and conforms to specification of USP, FCC, JP,BP, ETC.

The Company Logo called **"SWASTIK"** is a religious symbol in India representing Truth and Non-Violence.

MEMBERSHIP:

American Chemical Society , USA

National Soft Drinks Association, USA

FIGURE 2.7   The Swastika: A Different Cultural Perspective

Symbols: The Swastika

For many people, the swastika is associated primarily with the genocidal 20th-century Nazi movement (Figure 2.8). However, for millions of Hindus, it is the symbol of good luck and well-being (Figure 2.9). For Hindus, swastika comes from Sanskrit, meaning "good luck" or "well-being"; more literally, "it is good." If it is drawn clockwise, it represents the evolution of the universe (*Pravritti*); anti-clockwise, it represents the involution of the universe (*Nivritti*). Hindus all over India still use the symbol in both representations for the sake of balance, although the standard form is the left-facing swastika. Buddhists almost always use the left-facing swastika.

The Nazis, who believed that the early Aryans of India (from whose Vedic tradition the swastika sprang) were the prototypical white invaders, saw fit to co-opt the sign as a symbol of white unity. It has come to signify fascism outside of India due to its history in World War II (*www.wikipedia.com*).

FIGURE 2.8   Nazi Swastika

FIGURE 2.9   Hindu Swastika

Similarly, when designing web sites for Eastern cultures like Japan and China, it should be noted that such cultures place special value on nature symbolism. Nature symbolism is extensively used as an aesthetic expression in Eastern cultures. For example, in China and Japan, nature symbols like mountains, rivers, birds, trees, and so on are commonly used in advertising, packaging, and even on web sites.

Also, it is important to use local or ethnically compatible human models, pictures, and images on web sites. For example, the international web sites of IKEA, MTV, Seven Eleven, and Sony have incorporated local models and celebrities from specific local cultures.

Icons

Several icons are specific to countries or areas in the world. When analyzing a web site, special attention is needed to know whether the icon is understood in a particular culture. For example, the icons of a yellow school bus, a red hexagonal sign, an American mailbox with a flag, a trash can, or a shopping cart may not be well understood outside the United States. Thus, when using icons on the web page, country-specific understanding is needed.

Icon Misunderstanding

Customers in Britain found the trashcan icon in the Apple Macintosh "trash can" very confusing, because it was a cylindrical bin, shaped exactly like mail boxes in Britain. In this case, it was particularly difficult because mail was mistakenly being sent to the trash can.

Color Symbolism

Different colors mean different things to people in different cultures. For example, Ricks et al. (1974) gives an example of a company with packaging having a green label, which was not well received by some Malaysians because to them green symbolized the jungle with its dangers and diseases. However, green is a color of fertility in Egypt, a color symbolizing safety in the United States, and a color that indicates criminality in France (Barber and Badre 1998). Similarly, in Western cultures, white is the color for the bride's gown, whereas in India, widows traditionally wear white. Different color combinations also carry different meanings in different cultures. For example, in China black on red is a symbol of happiness and is widely used on wedding invitations, while in Japan red over white signifies celebration and life force. Thus, use of specific colors and color combinations on the web sites has to be congruent with the needs and expectations of a specific country. (For more details on colors and cultures, see the Global Color Chart in Appendix 2.2 at the end of this chapter.)

BEHAVIOR AND CULTURE

At the behavioral level of cultural analysis, it is important to understand what forces make us behave and react the way we do. According to Trompenaars (1994), norms and values guide our actions and aspirations; in fact, cultural values guide individuals concerning preferable modes of conduct or end states of existence (Pollay 1983).

In the field of marketing, cultural values have been recognized to have a significant impact on consumer motivations, product choices, and lifestyles (Cheng and Schweitzer 1996; Tse, Belk, and Zhou 1989). For example, the popular Information-Processing Model of Consumer Behavior explicitly recognizes culture as an external factor impacting consumer decision-making. However, in the context of global markets and global consumers, more and more researchers (e.g., Mooij 2003) emphasize that culture is not just an external factor, but an integral part of all human behavior and thus, consumer behavior too. We will spend the next five chapters focusing on the "behavior" aspect of culture, and draw important conclusions for web site design.

We should emphasize that even though the coming chapters focus entirely on cultural behavior and its ramifications to web sites, the reader should not overlook the perception and symbolism aspects of culture discussed in this chapter. The issues of *perception* and *symbolism* will always have to be kept in mind when web sites are designed, even as one focuses on the *behavior* aspects of culture of a target market. As such, a culturally customized web site should always address all three aspects of cultures: perception, symbolism, and behavior.

Visit www.theculturallycustomizedwebsite.com for additional information and updates.

CHAPTER KEYS

For those managing web sites, a key statistic of interest is web ROI—the return on web investment.

Web ROI depends on persuading visitors to take the action you want them to take; research indicates this persuasion effort is greatly strengthened if visitors feel "at home," with web site attributes that are culturally consistent and familiar.

Three factors play important roles in culture: perception, symbolism, and behavior.

Perception is governed by many variables, but three that are of relevance to web sites are the environment, language, and color. They influence the spatial orientation of the content, text length, navigational modes, translation equivalence, language dialects, and color categories.

Symbolism is the system of representations and symbols. Symbols are the vehicles through which cultural information is passed from one generation to the other. It has obvious implications to web site design as web sites abound in images, icons, and color symbolism.

The issue of cultural behavior is crucial to global business as culture molds taste and affects perception. Thus, it impacts purchase behavior and hence revenue and profits. The rest of the book will focus on various aspects of culture as it relates to behavior.

EXERCISES

Students

(1) The chapter includes a discussion on how different cultures "slice" the color spectrum in different ways (see page 32). For example, most Western cultures break-up the rainbow into seven colors: violet, indigo, blue green, yellow, orange, and red (VIBGYOR). Find a person from another culture

(e.g., an international student) and ask him or her to write down the colors of the rainbow in his or her language. Next find another individual from the same culture to translate the colors to English. Do they conform to VIBGYOR?

(2) Use an idiom in a sentence (page 35 lists commonly used idioms in the United States); ask an individual from a different country to translate that sentence, after you have explained to him what the idiom means. Take this translated sentence and have it back-translated in English by another individual from the same country. Is the back-translated sentence consistent with your original sentence?

Managers

Pick any one of your international web sites (or your home web site that draws international consumers). List every color on the site. Refer to the *Global Color Chart* (see Appendix 2.2) and examine if any of your colors would be insensitive to any cultural group among your customers (e.g., white signifies death in many Eastern cultures, whereas death is symbolized by black in the West) or inconsistent to their world (e.g., Swedish mailboxes are yellow, whereas they are red in most parts of the world.)

APPENDIX 2.1

Details of the study discussed on page 26 are presented below.

The results in general show that Local Web Sites generated stronger purchase intention and more positive attitude toward the site. Post hoc tests provide further support that Local Web Sites were preferred over Adapted and Standardized Web Sites (Singh, Furrer, and Massimilaino 2004).

TABLE 2.3   MANOVA Results and Post Hoc Group Comparisons

	Type of web site[a]				Tukey test[b]
Measures	Local	Adapted	Standard	F	Group comparisons[c]
Italy					
Attitude toward site	3.72	3.41	3.38	5.35**	L>A; L>S
Purchase intention	3.17	2.89	2.82	3.71**	L>S
India					
Attitude toward site	3.90	3.85	3.27	15.6**	S<L & A
Purchase intention	3.90	3.64	3.35	13.8**	L>A>S

Continues

TABLE 2.3   MANOVA Results and Post Hoc Group Comparisons—cont'd

Measures	Type of web site[a]			F	Tukey test[b] Group comparisons[c]
	Local	Adapted	Standard		
Switzerland					
Attitude toward site	2.98	3.15	3.06	ns	
Purchase intention	3.08	2.91	2.64	3.24*	L>S
Spain					
Attitude toward site	4.04	3.46	3.01	12.7**	L>A & S
Purchase intention	3.89	3.30	2.81	14.1**	L>A>S

[a]Mean values are reported; * $p < .05$; $^{**}p < .01$

[b]Comparisons that are significant at $< .05$ level are reported.

[c]L=Local web site, A=Adapted web site, S=Standardized web site (Singh, Zhao, and Hu 2004).

Singh N., Furrer O., and Massimilaino O. (2004) To Localize or to Standardize on the Web: Empirical Evidence from Italy, India, Netherlands, Switzerland, and Spain, *Multinational Business Review*, 12(1), 69–88.

APPENDIX 2.2

Global Color Chart

(From Beyond Borders, by John Yunker [Yunker 2003]; used with permission)

Colors mean different things to different people. Sometimes, colors mean different things to different cultures. Table 2.4, which is compiled from many sources, will give you an idea of the range of meanings a color can have. It is by no means definitive, nor is it prescriptive.

The meaning of color is like the meaning of language: constantly evolving and usually open to interpretation. The meaning of a color can vary not only between cultures but also within cultures. A color might even have two contradictory meanings. For example, in the United States, a person dressed in black may be going to a funeral or to a dance club. Context plays a critical role in defining color, as does the combination of colors. In France, the combination of blue, white, and red in the national flag signifies *liberté*, *égalité*, and *fraternité*, respectively. In the United States, the same three colors are also used in the flag, but the meanings are slightly different.

TABLE 2.4   Global Color Chart

Region	Significance	Example
Red		
U.S.	Excitement, warning, sex, passion, spicy, valor	Stop signs, fire trucks
Mexico	Religion, vibrancy, death	Aztec color for the north, national flag
Brazil	Visibility, vibrancy	Red cars illegal in Brazil and Ecuador because of the perception that they cause more accidents

Continues

TABLE 2.4   Global Color Chart—cont'd

Region	Significance	Example
Greece	Love, autumn, good luck	Wine, eggs dyed red for Easter for luck
U.K.	Authority, power, government, visibility	Mailboxes, buses, telephone booths
Africa	Death, bloodshed	Mourning clothing
China, Hong Kong, Taiwan	Communism, celebration, good luck, joy, fertility	Wedding dresses, lucky money envelopes, red ink used in obituaries
Japan	Blood, passion, self-sacrifice, strength	Public phones, color of flag (rising sun)
India	Birth, fertility	Wedding dress, henna color in hair
Scandinavia	Strength	Eric the Red
Blue		
U.S.	Justice, perseverance, trust, official business	Uniforms, mailboxes, color of flag, color of the Chief Executive
Scandinavia	Cleanliness	Hospital supplies
India	Heavens, love, truth	Krishna's skin
Greece	National pride	Color of flag
Israel	Holiness	In ancient history, priestly garments were dyed with a blue ink obtained from a now-extinct sea creature known as the Chilazon
Germany	Loyalty, formality	Government letters traditionally are mailed in blue envelopes
White		
U.S.	Purity, innocence, virginity	Bedding, hospital uniforms
U.K.	Leisure, sports	Sportswear
China, Hong Kong, Taiwan	Death, mourning, purity	Funeral clothing, packages
India	Death, rebirth, serenity	Brahman (highest caste)
Africa	Victory, purity	School uniforms of young girls
Black		
U.S.	Death, sophistication, formality	Color of mourning, formal wear
U.K.	Death, formality	Formal wear, color of taxis
Brazil	Sophistication, mourning, formality	Formal clothing, mourning clothing, religious clothing
Mexico	Mourning, respect	Clerical robes
Germany	Death, grief, hopelessness, formality	Clergy attire, black automobiles of government ministers
Green		
U.S.	Environmental, freshness, health inexperience, envy	Money, nature, highway signs, being "green with envy"
Ireland	Catholicism, nationalism	National color

TABLE 2.4   Global Color Chart—cont'd

Region	Significance	Example
Germany	Hope, conservation	Police uniforms
Arab Middle East	Holiness	Holy color of Islam; the Prophet Muhammad wore a green turban, and green is believed to have been his favorite color. Mosques are frequently decorated with green tiles.
Yellow		
U.S.	Visibility, caution, faith	Police area, color of taxis, yellow ribbon as symbol for loved one to return home
Scandinavia	Warmth	Mailboxes in Sweden
India	Commerce	Taxis
Germany	Envy, jealousy	Germans use the phrase "yellow with envy"
Israel	Saintliness	Halo of God
Purple		
U.S.	Nobility, law, bravery	Purple Heart, collegiate colors
Latin America	Death	Purple flowers sent to funerals
Italy	Color of the church, authority	Used by high-ranking officials and the Catholic Church

REFERENCES

Barber, W. and Badre, A. (1998) Culturability: The Merging of Culture and Usability, *www.research.att.com/conf/hfweb/*

Berlin, B. and Kay, P. (1969) Basic Color Terms: Their Universality and Evolution, Berkeley, CA: University of California Press.

Berry, J.W., Poortinga, Y.H., Segall, M.H., and Dasen, P.R. (1992) Cross-Cultural Psychology: Research and Applications. Cambridge University Press.

Casson, R. (1983) Schemata in Cognitive anthropology, *Annual Review of Anthropology*, (12), 429–462.

Cheng, H. and Schweitzer, J.C. (1996) Cultural Values Reflected in Chinese and U.S Television Commercials, *Journal of Advertising Research*, (36) 3, 27–45.

Collins Concise Spanish Dictionary (2002). HarperCollins Publishers.

Csikszentmihalyi, M. (2000) *Beyond Boredom and Anxiety: Experiencing Flow in Work and Play*. San Francisco: Jossey-Bass.

Csikszentmihalyi, M. and LeFevre, J. (1989) Optimal Experience in Work and Leisure, *Journal of Personality and Social Psychology*, 56(5), 815–822.

D'Andrade, R.G. (1992) Schemas and Motivation. In *Human Motives and Cultural Models*, (eds;). R.G, D'Andrade, C., Strauss, N. Quinn, Cambridge University Press.

Deregowski, T.B. (1980) Perception. In H.C. Triandis and W. Lenner (eds.), The Handbook of Cross-Cultural Psychology, Vol. 3, 21–115. Boston: Allyn and Bacon.

Detweiler, R.A. (1978) Culture, Category Width, and Attributions, *Journal of Cross-Cultural Psychology*, 9(3), 259–284.

Fink, D. and Laupase, R. (2000) Perceptions of Web Site Design Characteristics: A Malaysian/Australian Comparison, *Internet Research*, Bradford; 10(1), 44–55.

Fock, H. (2000) Cultural Influences on Marketing Communication on the World Wide Web, *Paper Presented at the Multicultural Marketing Conference*, Hong Kong, Sept.

Geertz, C. (1973) *The Interpretation of Cultures*, New York: Basic Books.

Goodenough, W.H. (1981) *Culture, Language, and Society*. Menlo Park, CA: Benjamin/Cummings Publishing.

Hall, E.T. (1976) *Beyond Culture*. Garden City, NY: Doubleday.

Kale, S.H. (1991) Culture-Specific Marketing Communication: An Analytical Approach, *International Marketing Review*, 8(2), 18–30.

Kaplan, R.B. (1966) Cultural Thought and Patterns in Inter-Cultural Education, *Language Learning*, 16, 1–20.

Kroeber, A.L. and Kluckhohn, F. (1952) *Culture: A Critical Review of Concepts and Definitions*, New York: Vintage Books.

Levine, R.V. (1988) The Pace of Life across Cultures. In J.E. McGrath (ed.), The Social Psychology of Time, 39–60. Newbury Park, CA: Sage Publications.

Levy, S. (1959) Symbols for Sale, *Harvard Business Review*, 37(July/Aug), 117–125.

Luhmann, N. (1988) Familiarity, Confidence, and Trust. In D. Gambetta (ed.), Trust: Making and Breaking Cooperative Relationships, 94–107. Oxford, England: Blackwell.

Luna, D., Peracchio, L.A., and Juan, M.D. de (2002) Cross-Cultural and Cognitive Aspects of Web Site Navigation, *Journal of the Academy of Marketing Science*, 30(4), 397–410.

Lynch, P.D., Kent, R.J., and Srinivasan, S.S. (2001) The Global Internet Shopper: Evidence from Shopping Tasks in Twelve Countries, *Journal of Advertising Research*, 41(3), 15–23.

McCracken, G. (1986) Culture and Consumption: A Theoretical Account of the Structure and Movement of the Cultural Meaning of Consumer Goods, *Journal of Consumer Research*, 13(June), 71–84.

Mick, D.G. (1986) Consumer Research and Semiotics: Exploring the Morphology of Signs, Symbols, and Significance, *Journal of Consumer Research*, 13(Sept), 196–213.

Mooij, M. de (2003) Consumer Behavior and Culture: Consequences for Global Marketing and Advertising, The Netherlands: Cross Cultural Communications Company.

Mooij, M. de (2004) Consumer Behavior and Culture, Thousand Oaks, CA: Sage Publications.

Pollay, R.W. (1983) Measuring the Cultural Values Manifest in Advertising. In J.H. Leigh and C.R. Martin (eds.), *Current Issues and Research in Advertising*, 72–92. Ann Arbor: MI: University of Michigan Press.

Quinn, N. and Holland, D. (1987), Culture and Cognition. In: *Cultural Models in Language and Thought*, eds. D. Holland and N.Quinn, London: Cambridge Univ. Press, 3–40.

Radzievsky, Y. and Radzievsky, A. (1998) Successful Global Web Sites Look Through Eyes of the Audience, *Advertising Age's Business Marketing*, 83(Jan), 17.

Rockwell, B. (1998) *Using the Web to compete in a Global Marketplace*. John Wiley & Sons

Rokeach, M. (1979) Understanding Human Values: Individual and Societal. New York: Free Press.

Ricks, D.R, Arpan, J.S. and Fu, M.Y. (1974) Pitfalls in Advertising Overseas, *Journal of Advertising Research*, 14(6), 47–51.

Sakade, F., ed. (1982) A Guide to Reading and Writing Japanese. Tokyo: Charles E. Tuttle.

Sapir, E. (1929) The Status of Linguistics as a Science. In E. Sapir (1958) *Culture, Language and Personality* (D. G. Mandelbaum, ed.). Berkeley, CA: University of California Press.

Segal, M.H., Campbell, D.T., and Herskovits, M.J. (1966) *Influence of Culture on Visual Perception*. Indianapolis, IN: Bobbs-Merrill Company Inc.

Shenkar, O. and von Glinow, M.A. (1994) Paradoxes of Organizational Theory and Research: Using the Case of China to Illustrate National Contingency, Management Science, 40(1), 56–71.

Simon, S.J. (1999) A Cross Cultural Analysis of Web Site Design: An Empirical Study of Global Web Users, *Paper Presented at the Seventh Cross-Cultural Consumer and Business Studies Research Conference*, Cancun, Mexico.

Simon, S.J. (2001) The Impact of Culture and Gender on Web Sites: An Empirical Study, *Database for Advances in Information Systems*, 32(1), 18–37.

Singer, M.R. (1998) *Perception and Identity in Intercultural communication*. Intercultural Press Inc.

Singh, N. (2003) Analyzing Cultural Sensitivity of Web Sites: A Normative Framework, Journal of Practical Global Business, 2(Spring), *www.expandglobal.com/journal/Jour_2/journalvI_2.htm*

Singh, N. (2004) From Cultural Models to Cultural Categories: A Framework for Cultural Analysis, *Journal of American Academy of Business*, Cambridge, 5(1–2), 95–102.

Singh, N., Furrer, O., and Massimilaino O. (2004) To Localize or to Standardize on the Web: Empirical Evidence from Italy, India, Netherlands, Switzerland, and Spain, *Multinational Business Review*, 12-(1), 69–88.

Shweder and R.A. Le Vine (eds.), Culture Theory: Essay on Mind, Self, and Emotion, 88–119. Cambridge University Press.

Triandis, H.C. (1972) *The Analysis of Subjective Culture*. New York: John Wiley.

Triandis, H.C. (1982) Review of Culture's Consequences: International Differences in Work-Related Values, *Human Organization*, 41, 86–90.

Trompenaars, F. (1994) *Riding the Waves of Culture: Understanding Diversity in Global Business*. New York: Irwin Professional Publishing.

Turnage, T.W. and McGinnies, E. (1973) A Cross-Cultural Comparison of the Effects of Presentation Mode and Meaningfulness on Short-Term Recall, *American Journal of Psychology*, 86(2), 369–381.

Tse, D.K., Belk, R.W., and Zhou, N. (1989) Becoming a Consumer Society: A Longitudinal and Cross-Cultural Content Analysis of Print Ads from Hong Kong, The People's Republic of China, and Taiwan, *Journal of Consumer Research*, 15(March), 457–472.

Usunier, J.-C. (1999) The Use of Language in Investigating Conceptual Equivalence in Cross-Cultural Research. In G. Albaum and S.M. Smith (eds.), *Proceedings of the Seventh Cross-Cultural Consumer and Business Studies Research Conference*, Cancun, Mexico, 12–15 December 1999.

Wassman, J. and Dasen, P. (1998) Balinese Spatial Orientation, *Journal of Royal Anthropological Institute* 4(4), 689–713.

Yunker, J. (2003) Beyond Borders: *Web Globalization Strategies*. Indianapolis, IN: New Riders.

3

A CULTURAL VALUES FRAMEWORK FOR WEB DESIGN

In this chapter, we provide a Cultural Values Framework, *drawn from well-established cultural research; these unique values encompass global cultures and have direct implications for customizing web sites for a specific culture of interest. We also discuss the implications of using countries as a basis for selecting cultural values, and we provide evidence of the validity of using our proposed cultural values framework in web site design.*

CHAPTER HIGHLIGHTS

CULTURAL BEHAVIOR

DEFINITIONS OF CULTURAL VALUES AND THEIR IMPLICATIONS

CULTURES AND COUNTRIES

CULTURAL VALUES FRAMEWORK: IMPLICATIONS FOR WEB SITES

VALIDITY OF THE CULTURAL VALUES FRAMEWORK

CULTURAL BEHAVIOR

The previous chapter introduced three key aspects of culture: *perception, symbolism,* and *behavior,* and provided an overview of perception and symbolism as they relate to web design. In this chapter—and the chapters that follow—we focus on behavior that is based on culture, and its implications for web site design.

Based on our research, we offer an empirically validated, theoretically sound framework comprised of five unique cultural values that account for similarities and differences across global cultures. Our research was done in three steps: First, we completed an extensive review of major cultural typologies[1] in

1. The works of Feather (1990, 1995), Hall and Hall (1990), Hofstede (1980, 1991), Kluckhohn and Strodtbeck (1961), Pollay (1983), Rokeach (1973), Triandis (1972, 1994) and Trompenaars (1994) were consulted.

the academic literature. Second, we reviewed research that operationalized these typologies and empirically tested them.[2] Finally, we evaluated the major cultural typologies in the context of web communication. Based on this three-step procedure, we arrived at a Cultural Values Framework using Hofstede's (1980) and Hall's (1976) cultural dimensions.

A key aspect for the choice of Hofstede is that his work is based on the earlier writings of Parsons and Shils (1951)—whose approach accommodates not only behavior, but also perception and symbolism. Hofstede (1980) used the work of Parsons and Shils (1951), among others,[3] and developed what is now a well-known, validated, and widely used cultural classification.

The five unique values that comprise our framework are as follows:

Individualism-Collectivism
Power Distance
Uncertainty Avoidance
Masculinity-Femininity
Low-High Context

The first four are drawn from Hofstede (1980), and the fifth is based on Hall's (1976) work.

DEFINITIONS OF CULTURAL VALUES AND THEIR IMPLICATIONS

Individualism-Collectivism: A belief in the importance of the goals of the individual (individualism) versus the goals of the group (collectivism). This value indicates how closely or loosely a society is knit. In individualistic cultures, the needs, values, and goals of an individual take precedence over group goals; the opposite is true for collectivistic cultures.

Power Distance: A belief in authority and hierarchy (high power distance) versus the belief that power should be distributed (low power distance). Cultures high on power distance accept power and hierarchy in the society and are low on egalitarianism. In such cultures, less powerful citizens are accepting of unequal power distribution in society.

Uncertainty Avoidance: The importance of predictability, structure, and order (high uncertainty avoidance) versus a willingness for risk-taking and an acceptance of ambiguity and limited structure (low uncertainty avoidance.) People from cultures high on uncertainty avoidance tend to have low toler-

2. Albers-Miller and Gelb 1996; Cheng and Schewitzer 1996; Borden 1991; Fock 2000; Gregory and Munch 1997; Gudykunst 1998; Han and Shavitt 1994; McCarty and Hattwick 1992; Mueller 1987; Tansey, Hyman, and Zinkhan 1990; Triandis 1982; Tse, Belk, and Zhou 1989; Zandpour et al. 1994.

3. Besides Parsons and Shils (1951), Hofstede consulted the works of other thinkers such as Kluckhohn and Strodtbeck (1961) and Inkeles and Levinson (1969).

ance for uncertainty and avoid ambiguous situations, view conflict and competition as threatening, and value security over adventure and risk.

Masculinity-Femininity: A belief in achievement and ambition (masculine) versus a belief in nurturing and caring for others (feminine). Masculine cultures value assertiveness, material possessions, and success, while feminine cultures place more value on helping others, preserving the environment, quality of life, and nurturance.

High-Low Context: High context cultures have close connections among group members, and everybody knows what every other person knows. Thus, in such cultures most of the information to function in a group is intrinsically known, and there is little information that is explicit. High context cultures use more symbols and nonverbal cues to communicate, with meanings embedded in the situational context. Low context cultures are societies that are logical, linear, action-oriented, and the mass of the information is explicit and formalized. Most of the communication in such cultures takes place in a rational, verbal, and explicit way to convey concrete meanings through rationality and language.

Hofstede's four cultural dimensions capture the essence of values most commonly observed across cultures (Hofstede 1980, 1991). They are empirically derived and have been shown to be sensitive to regional differences (Cho et al., 1999) and are particularly robust when used as a single source to explain diversity in consumption behavior and ownership of products (Mooij 2000). More relevant, these cultural value dimensions touch the perceptual, behavioral, and symbolic levels. For example, they have been used to study the user's perception of web sites (Simon 1999), and they have been used to study symbolic content and advertisement appeals in the advertising media (Albers-Miller and Gelb 1996; Cho et al. 1999). In essence, these cultural values represent the most basic and core beliefs of a society encompassing the perceptual, symbolic, and behavioral elements of culture.

While there has been some criticism for Hofstede's cultural typology regarding methodology and context (Huang 1995), it can be argued that Hofstede's typology is appropriate for several reasons. First, Hofstede's cultural typology has been extensively replicated showing it to be an important part of cultural theory. Second, according to Clark (1990), there seems to be an overlap among different typologies of culture offered by other researchers, and in many cases, their dimensions correspond to Hofstede's typology. Finally, Hofstede's typology has been found to be a valid basis for analysis of regional differences and a means through which web marketers could adapt their web sites to local cultures (Simon 1999).

Hall's work on high/low context has been validated by various researchers, particularly with regard to advertising and promotion within cultures. Advertisements in high context cultures are characterized by indirect verbal expressions and are implicit and indirect, polite, modest, and even ambiguous (Mooij 1998; Mueller 1987). In a low context environment, the use of direct, explicit, and confrontational appeals in the form of competitive advertising, sales promotions, and aggressive selling is common (Cutler and Javalgi 1992; Mueller 1987). Thus, while communication in high context cultures is implicit, indirect, and deeply embedded in the context, the communication in low context cultures is more direct, less implicit, and more informative.

Researchers have rated and ranked various countries on Hofstede's cultural values. Thus, given a country (e.g., the United States), one can check its score on a particular cultural value (e.g., individualism) as well as its ranking on that cultural value vis-à-vis other countries. *Appendix 3.1 provides a listing of various country scores on Hofstede's cultural dimensions and their ranking vis-à-vis the other countries.* As such, a country's score on the cultural dimensions indicates a particular cultural pre-disposition, and this has been validated by research. For example, high power distance cultures like Mexico and Malaysia use status symbols more frequently than low power distance cultures. According to Mooij (1998, pp.186–188), it is common to see the elder advising the younger, and the "boss" is frequently admired in these cultures. The people of low power distance cultures, like Sweden and Denmark, desire appeals based on independence and related themes, and humor is widely used (Mooij 1998). Appeals used in individualistic societies, like the United States and Great Britain, are more personalized than in collectivistic societies. Consider L'Oreal's advertising campaign "Because you're worth it," or Nike's slogan "Just do it." In collectivistic societies, an indirect approach is favored. Appeals like "It's so good, you want to share it with others" and "Working together" are more common in these cultures (Mooij 1998). In Masculine cultures, appeals are based on effectiveness, convenience, and productivity, whereas in Feminine cultures, appeals tend to be based on nature, frailty, and modesty (Albers-Miller and Gelb 1996). In high uncertainty avoidance cultures, there is a greater need for explanations, structure, and expert testimonials compared to low uncertainty avoidance cultures (Mooij 1998). Credible, familiar, and attractive sources for communication can be effective appeals in high uncertainty avoidance cultures. Symbolic association, on the other hand, is likely to be less effective in high uncertainty avoidance cultures because it lacks clear direction and linear logic (Zandpour et al. 1994).

CULTURES AND COUNTRIES

A relevant question at this juncture is the following: Can we assume that countries are homogenous bastions of specific cultures, as indicated by Appendix 3.1? For example, based on Appendix 3.1, can one claim that all Americans are individualistic and that all Chinese are collectivistic? The answer is obviously no; however, it is fair to say that in general, Americans are individualistic and Chinese, collectivistic.

More importantly, as people migrate between countries and cultures, we expect acculturation takes place—research studies confirm this, revealing that the time and degree of acculturation vary from individual to individual. Thus, a

Chinese immigrant to the United States will become acculturated over time, meaning that the individual will become more and more individualistic. The reasoning for this is straightforward: it is unlikely that one can migrate to, and succeed in, a country by rejecting or refusing to accept its core cultural values. As such, culture is an adaptive process and newcomers to a country undergo this process. People undergoing acculturation are in a constant state of flux (Ogden, Ogden, and Schau 2004) and at any given point in time there are individuals at various levels of acculturation, meaning that at any juncture, there are various subcultures existing in a given country. Wal-Mart took advantage of this situation very successfully in Colorado by targeting Latino fans of the Denver Broncos (the football team) who were at various levels of acculturation. They introduced two styles of Denver Broncos T-shirts: one with the helmet logo featuring an air-brushed sheen and another featuring the phrase *de todo corazon* (with all my heart). These T-shirts were the hottest Broncos merchandise of the 2003 season (*Marketing News* 2004). We would expect the next generation of these Latino fans of the Denver Broncos to be culturally more American, even as new Latino immigrants come in to take their place in the acculturation process.

Thus, even as we view countries as homogenous cultural "units," we acknowledge that there will always be various subcultures within a country. However, the existence of these subcultures does little to detract from the broad cultural homogeneity reflected in the *behavior* of the vast majority of a country's residents—particularly *consumer behavior*. There is a substantial body of research that indicates the existence of behavioral differences in consumers, across countries.[4] For example, a recent study investigating service marketing in Australia, China, Germany, India, Morocco, and the Netherlands showed clear cultural differences in consumer behavior across the eight countries (Thomas, Hult, Kandemir, and Keillor 2004).

Hence, it is useful to view countries on the five cultural values (as seen in Appendix 3.1) and to decide web strategy based on these cultural differences. Further, if there are substantial subcultures in existence, it may be wise to act on that knowledge too. Specifically, businesses targeting a particular country should (1) identify the country's broad cultural values, and (2) identify the existence (if any) of other subcultures in the country that may be of relevance to the company. As an example, a company targeting the United Kingdom may recognize the existence of a substantial and relevant Indian subculture within the country and may want to reach out to it. That would indicate the need to have *two* culturally customized web sites for the UK market: one customized on the United Kingdom's cultural values and one customized on India's cultural values. If the company already has a separate web site for India, that site can be used to target the Indian subculture in the United Kingdom, as long as there is easy access to that site from the UK web site and that customers in the UK can have the ability to make purchases, access customer services, and so forth from either web site.

---

4. Brass 1991; McCarty and Hattwick 1991.

The above discussion can be extended to include key implications for the future. In an increasingly globalized world where country borders are being erased, and there is free flow of commerce, labor, and information, it may not be sufficient to target country markets in the future, as we do today. It is likely that—in the future—under such widely globalized conditions, it would be preferable to target the specific cultures of free-flowing, migrating masses of people. Thus, future customers should be able to access a master web site for a company and then pick the site that appeals to them and satisfies their specific cultural needs.

CULTURAL VALUES FRAMEWORK: IMPLICATIONS FOR WEB SITES

To generate operational web site features for the various values in the cultural framework, we created a list of all major interactive or multimedia features commonly present on web sites (e.g., clubs, newsletters, FAQs, security policy, privacy policy, free stuff, downloads, graphics, hyperlinks, and others) and then evaluated these features vis-à-vis the five cultural dimensions. Thus, we would expect features that tend to emphasize community features such as chat rooms, clubs, community newsletters, and family-oriented themes to be consistent with collectivism, whereas in the case of individualism, emphasis would be needed on self-direction options, individual customization, and themes reflecting independence and materialism.

To help identify all relevant features and aid in the categorization, the work of Albers-Miller and Gelb (1996) was consulted, as they empirically tested the extent to which various cultural values appeals by Pollay (1983) are reflective of each of Hofstede's four dimensions. Other studies that have used and operationalized Hofstede's and Hall's typology were also evaluated (Cheng and Schweitzer 1996; Cho et al. 1999; Mueller 1987). The resulting list of web features that was chosen for analysis (see Singh and Matsuo 2004; Singh, Zhao, and Hu 2003) are listed in Appendix 3.2. The features listed in Appendix 3.2 were then analyzed and categorized into the relevant cultural value dimensions by four independent judges.[5] The resulting categories of features are presented in Table 3.1 (Singh and Baack 2004; Singh and Matsuo 2004; Singh, Zhao, and Hu 2003).

---

5. A total interjudge reliability of 83 percent was achieved. To further test the reliability and minimize intercorrelations between the categories, a study of 150 American, Chinese, Indian, Mexican, and Japanese web sites was conducted. The aim of the study was to test the reliability of the cultural dimensions and check for conceptual overlap. In summary, some category items were deleted due to conceptual overlap, and some web elements were deleted as they were found to be part of global web culture, such as security policy, privacy statement, country news, and so on (Singh, Zhao, and Hu 2003; Singh and Matsuo 2004).

Text continued on page 61

TABLE 3.1 Web Features and Cultural Values

Value: Collectivism

Community Relations: A community policy, giving back to community, social responsibility policy.

Clubs/Chat Rooms: Members club, product-based clubs, chat with interest groups, message boards, discussion groups, and live talks.

Newsletter: Online subscriptions, magazines, and newsletters.

Family Theme: Pictures of family, pictures of teams of employees, mention of employee teams and emphasis on team and collective work responsibility in vision statement or elsewhere on the web site, and emphasis on customers as a family.

Symbols and Pictures of National Identity: Flags, pictures of historic monuments, pictures reflecting uniqueness of the country, country-specific symbols in the form of icons, and indexes.

Loyalty Programs: Customer loyalty programs, company credit cards for specific country, and special membership programs.

Links to Local Web Sites: Links to local partners, related country-specific companies, and other local web sites from a particular country.

Value: Individualism

Good Privacy Statement: Privacy policy and how personal information will be protected or used.

Independence Theme: Images and themes depicting self-reliance, self-recognition, and achievement.

Product Uniqueness: Unique selling points of the product and product differentiation features.

Personalization: Gift recommendations, individual acknowledgments or greetings, and web page personalization

Value: Uncertainty Avoidance

Customer Service: FAQs, customer service options, customer help, customer contact, or customer service e-mails.

Guided Navigation: Site maps, well-displayed links, links in the form of pictures or buttons, forward, backward, up and down navigation buttons.

Tradition Theme: Emphasis on history and ties of a particular company with a nation, emphasis on respect, veneration of elderly and the culture, phrases like "most respected company," "keeping the tradition alive," "for generations," and "company legacy."

Local Stores: Mention of contact information for local offices, dealers, and shops.

Local Terminology: Use of country-specific metaphors, names of festivals, puns, and a general local touch to the vocabulary of the web page, not just mere translation.

Free Trials or Downloads: Free stuff, free downloads, free screen savers, free product trials, free coupons to try the products or services, free memberships, or free service information.

Toll-Free Numbers: Telephone access around the clock.

Transaction Security and Testimonials: Testimonials from customers, trust-enhancing features like reliability seals, seals of trust, and ethical business practices from third parties.

Continues

TABLE 3.1   Web Features and Cultural Values—cont'd

Value: Power Distance

Company Hierarchy Information: Information about the ranks of company personnel, information about organizational chart, and information about country managers.

Pictures of CEOs: Pictures of executives, important people in the industry, or celebrities.

Quality Assurance and Awards: Mention of awards won, mention of quality assurance information and quality certification by international and local agencies.

Vision Statement: The vision for the company, as stated by the CEO or top management.

Pride of Ownership Appeal: Depiction of satisfied customers, fashion statement for the use of product, and the use of reference groups to portray pride.

Proper Titles: Titles of the important people in the company, titles of the people in the contact information, and titles of people on the organizational charts.

Value: Masculinity

Quizzes and Games: Games, quizzes, fun stuff to do on the web site, tips and tricks, recipes, and other such information.

Realism Theme: Less fantasy and imagery on the web site, to-the-point information.

Product Effectiveness: Durability information, quality information, product attribute information, and product robustness information.

Clear Gender Roles: Separate pages for men and women, depiction of women in nurturance roles, depiction of women in "traditional" positions of telephone operators, models, wives, and mothers; depiction of men as macho, strong, and in positions of power.

Value: High Context

Politeness and Indirectness: Greeting from the company, images and pictures reflecting politeness, flowery language, use of indirect words (e.g., "perhaps," "probably," "somewhat"), and overall humility in company philosophy and corporate information.

Soft-Sell Approach: Use of affective and subjective impressions of intangible aspects of a product or service and use of the entertainment theme to promote the product.

Aesthetics: Attention to aesthetic details, liberal use of colors, bold colors, emphasis on images and context, and use of love and harmony appeal.

Value: Low Context

Hard-Sell Approach: Aggressive promotions, discounts, coupons, and emphasis on product advantages using explicit comparison.

Use of Superlatives: Use of superlative words and sentences like "We are the number one," "The top company," "The leader," "World's largest."

Rank or Prestige of the Company: Features like company rank in the industry, listing or ranking in important media (e.g., Forbes or Fortune), and numbers showing the growth and importance of the company.

Terms and Condition of Purchase: Product return policy, warranty, and other conditions associated with the purchase.

Singh and Baack (2004), Singh and Matsuo (2004), Singh, Zhao and Hu (2003, 2004).

VALIDITY OF THE CULTURAL VALUES FRAMEWORK

To test the validity of the proposed Cultural Values Framework, we sampled web sites from four culturally diverse countries: China, India, Japan and the United States (scores of these countries on Hofstede-Hall values are shown in Table 3.2).

If our proposed framework is a valid one, we would expect business web sites of domestic companies in these countries to have the kind of features that are consistent with their respective cultures.

It is important to note that the existence of the relevant cultural features alone doesn't guarantee success for a web site; conversely, the lack of relevant features does not preclude success. However, we would expect that, in general, successful web sites targeting specific countries will tend to be culturally sensitive to their customers; thus, we would expect to see the existence of site features consistent with the culture of interest. Further, given that these values are on a continuum, each country has a mix of various values; as such we can expect to see, for example, collectivistic features even for a country that may have an "average" score on collectivism. However, we should expect that customers from cultures that exhibit a dominant cultural value would frequent those sites that exhibit features consistent with that cultural value.

The Study

The validation of the framework in these four countries is based on Singh, Zhao, and Hu (2004). The web sites for the analysis were chosen as follows: 25 Japanese and 26 U.S. company web sites were selected from the Forbes 500 (*www.forbes.com*); 21 Indian and 21 Chinese web sites were selected from the Yahoo Indian and Chinese directories. To control for industry effects, if any, only electronic and automotive companies were included in the sample. Thus, a total of 93 web sites (with an average of 18 web pages per site) were sampled and analyzed using a combination of qualitative and quantitative methods.

Methodology

First, the cultural content in the sampled web sites was evaluated. The degree of depiction of each of the 36 value items in the Cultural Value Framework was

TABLE 3.2   Hofstede-Hall Values for the United States, China, and India

Country	Individualism	Uncertainty avoidance	Power distance	Masculinity	Context
U.S.	91	43	40	62	Low
China	20	60	80	50	High
India	48	40	77	56	High/Low
Japan	46	92	54	95	High

evaluated as "Not Depicted" to "Prominently Depicted" on a five-point Likert scale, by two independent coders from each of the four countries. The percentage of agreement[6] method was used to determine the coefficient of inter-coder reliability[7] for the 35 category items. The inter-coder reliability for U.S. web sites was 82 percent; for Japanese Web sites, it was 80 percent; for Chinese web sites, it was 85 percent; and for the Indian web sites, it was 88 percent. To check the intra-judge reliability, the coders coded a random sample of 25 percent of each of the U.S., Indian, Chinese, and Japanese web sites again after a month. An intra-judge reliability score of 88 percent, 90 percent, 89 percent, and 85 percent was achieved for U.S., India, China, and Japan, respectively. The second stage of the study analysis included other statistical analysis (see Appendix 3.3).

The results indicate that web sites of India, China, Japan, and the United States reflect values consistent with those predicted by the cultural value framework. Web sites from collectivist cultures like China and Japan depicted clubs, newsletters, family themes, and country-specific symbols more prominently than did the other web sites. Web sites from the United States (an individualistic culture) featured high levels of product uniqueness and web page personalization. High power distance societies like Japan and India prominently depicted features like hierarchy information, pictures of important people, and a prominent vision statement. Highly masculine cultures such as Japan depicted clear gender roles and an emphasis on product effectiveness. Further, Japanese web sites also scored highest on high contextuality with a strong bias toward a soft-sell approach and liberal use of aesthetic drawings. On the other hand, web sites from low context cultures like the United States were characterized by a hard-sell approach and the depiction of company rankings. The chapters that follow focus on the five cultural values and attempts to explicate each one in the context of designing web sites.

Visit www.theculturallycustomizedwebsite.com for additional information and updates.

CHAPTER KEYS

The five values that explain global cultural behavior are (drawn from Hofstede and Hall): Individualism-Collectivism, Power Distance, Uncertainty Avoidance, Masculinity-Femininity, Low-High Context. Countries have been rated and ranked on these values.

The rationale for using countries as a basis to understanding cultures has its limitations but is still very useful for global managers.

The five values can be implemented with regard to cultural customization of web sites through 36 items that make up the Cultural Values Framework.

6. Percentage of Agreement measures the percentage of cases on which the coders agreed.
7. Coefficient of inter-coder reliability: percentage of cases on which both coders agree. Intra-coder reliability was done after a prolonged time interval by the same coder; the previous results were compared with the new results to gauge percentage of agreement.

EXERCISES

Students

Appendix 3.1 provides the scores for various countries on Hofstede's values. Choose any two values, for example, Individualism-Collectivism and Power Distance. Map the countries on a grid (one axis is Individualism-Collectivism and the other axis is Power Distance). The resulting graph will "cluster" countries that are similar on both dimensions. Do the same exercise with the other two values. Of all the countries listed, which countries would you say are culturally most similar using *all four values*?

Managers

If your company targets multiple countries, attempt to map them (on a grid, as described above) on two or three cultural values. Countries that group together on the four values will tend to need similar cultural themes for cultural customization, helping you achieve cost efficiencies in web design.[8]

APPENDIX 3.1

TABLE 3.3   Country Scores on Hofstede's Cultural Values

Country	Power distance	Individualism-collectivism	Masculinity-femininity	Uncertainty avoidance
Arab World**	80	38	52	68
Argentina	49	46	56	86
Australia	36	90	61	51
Austria	11	55	79	70
Belgium	65	75	54	94
Brazil	69	38	49	76
Canada	39	80	52	48
Chile	63	23	28	86
China	80′	15′	55′	40′
Colombia	67	13	64	80
Costa Rica	35	15	21	86
Czech Republic	35′	60′	45′	60′
Denmark	18	74	16	23
East Africa**	64	27	41	52
Ecuador	78	8	63	67
El Salvador	66	19	40	94

Continues

8. Singh N., Zhao H., and Hu X. (2003) Cultural Adaptation on the Web: A Study of American Companies' Domestic and Chinese Web Sites, *Journal of Global Information Management,* 11(3), 63–81. Parts used in the book with permission from Idea Group Inc.

TABLE 3.3   Country Scores on Hofstede's Cultural Values—cont'd

Country	Power distance	Individualism-collectivism	Masculinity-femininity	Uncertainty avoidance
Finland	33	63	26	59
France	68	71	43	86
Germany	35	67	66	65
Greece	60	35	57	112
Guatemala	95	6	37	101
Hong Kong	68	25	57	29
Hungary	45'	55'	79'	83'
India	77	48	56	40
Indonesia	78	14	46	48
Iran	58	41	43	59
Ireland	28	70	68	35
Israel	13	54	47	81
Italy	50	76	70	75
Jamaica	45	39	68	13
Japan	54	46	95	92
Malaysia	104	26	50	36
Mexico	81	30	69	82
Netherlands	38	80	14	53
New Zealand	22	79	58	49
Norway	31	69	8	50
Pakistan	55	14	50	70
Panama	95	11	44	86
Peru	64	16	42	87
Philippines	94	32	64	44
Poland	55'	60'	65'	78'
Portugal	63	27	31	104
Singapore	74	20	48	8
South Africa	49	65	63	49
South Korea	60	18	39	85
Spain	57	51	42	86
Sweden	31	71	5	29
Switzerland	34	68	70	58
Taiwan	58	17	45	69
Thailand	64	20	34	64
Turkey	66	37	45	85
United Kingdom	35	89	66	35
United States	40	91	62	46
Uruguay	61	36	38	100
Venezuela	81	12	73	76
West Africa**	77	20	46	54

'Estimated values

** *Arab World:* Egypt, Iraq, Kuwait Lebanon, Libya, Saudi Arabia, United Arab Emirates; *East Africa:* Ethiopia, Kenya, Tanzania, Zambia; *West Africa:* Ghana, Nigeria, Sierra Leone.

Source: Hofstede G. (2001) *Culture's Consequences: Comparing Values, Behaviors, Institutions, and Organizations.* Thousand Oaks, CA: Sage Publications.

Appendix 3.2

TABLE 3.4   Web Features and Cultural Values

List of web features used for categorization into the relevant cultural value dimensions (see page 58).

Newsletter: Online subscriptions, magazines, and newsletters.

Customer Service: FAQs, customer service options, customer help, customer contact, or customer service e-mails

Guided Navigation: Site maps, well-displayed links, links in the form of pictures or buttons, forward, backward, up and down navigation buttons.

Free Trials or Downloads: Free stuff, free downloads, free screen savers, free product trials, free coupons to try the products or services, free memberships, or free service information.

Toll-Free Numbers: Telephone access around the clock.

Company Hierarchy Information: Information about the ranks of company personnel, information about organizational chart, and information about country managers.

Personalization: Gift recommendations, individual acknowledgments or greeting, and web page personalization.

Family Theme: Pictures of family, pictures of teams of employees, mention of employee teams and emphasis on team and collective work responsibility in vision statement or elsewhere on the web site, and emphasis on customers as a family.

Transaction Security and Testimonials: Testimonials from customers, trust-enhancing features like reliability seals, seals of trust, and ethical business practices from third parties.

Clear Gender Roles: Separate pages for men and women, depiction of women in nurturance roles, depiction of women in "traditional" positions of telephone operators, models, wives, and mothers; depiction of men as macho, strong, and in positions of power.

Terms and Condition of Purchase: Product return policy, warranty, and other conditions associated with the purchase.

Politeness and Indirectness: Greeting from the company, images and pictures reflecting politeness, flowery language, use of indirect words (e.g., "perhaps," "probably" "somewhat"), and overall humility in company philosophy and corporate information.

Clubs/Chat Rooms: Members club, product-based clubs, chat with company people, chat with interest groups, message boards, discussion groups, and live talks.

Good Privacy Statement: Privacy policy and how personal information will be protected or used.

Soft-Sell Approach: Use of affective and subjective impressions of intangible aspects of a product or service, and more entertainment theme to promote the product.

Use of Superlatives: Use of superlative words and sentences like "We are the number one," "The top company," "The leader," " World's largest."

Loyalty Programs: Customer loyalty programs, company credit cards for specific country, and special membership programs.

Links to Local web sites: Links to local partners, related country-specific companies, and other local web sites from a particular country.

Aesthetics: Attention to aesthetic details, liberal use of colors, bold colors, emphasis on images and context, and use of love and harmony appeal.

Independence Theme: Images and themes depicting self-reliance, self-recognition, and achievement.

Tradition Theme: Emphasis on history and ties of a particular company with a nation, emphasis on respect, veneration of elderly and the culture, phrases like "most respected company," "keeping the tradition alive," "for generations," "company legacy."

Continues

TABLE 3.4   Web Features and Cultural Values—cont'd

Local Stores: Mention of contact information for local offices, dealers, and shops.

Vision Statement: The vision for the company, as stated by the CEO or top management.

Pride of Ownership Appeal: Depiction of satisfied customers, fashion statement for the use of product, and the use of reference groups to portray pride.

Symbols and Pictures of National Identity: Flags, pictures of historic monuments, pictures reflecting uniqueness of the country, country-specific symbols in the form of icons, and indexes.

Independence Theme: Images and themes depicting self-reliance, self-recognition, and achievement.

Pictures of CEOs: Pictures of executives, important people in the industry or celebrities.

Quality Assurance and Awards: Mention of awards won, mention of quality assurance information, and mention of quality certification by international and local agencies.

Rank or Prestige of the Company: Features like company rank in the industry, listing or ranking in important media (e.g., Forbes or Fortune), and numbers showing the growth and importance of the company.

Realism Theme: Less fantasy and imagery on the web site, to-the-point information.

Product Effectiveness: Durability information, quality information, product attribute information, and product robustness information.

Product Uniqueness: Unique selling points of the product and product differentiation features.

Quizzes and Games: Games, quizzes, fun stuff to do on the web site, tips and tricks, recipes, and other such information.

Community Relations: A community policy, giving back to community, social responsibility policy.

Hard-Sell Approach: Aggressive promotions, discounts, coupons and emphasis on product advantages using explicit comparison.

Local Terminology: Use of country-specific metaphors, names of festivals, puns, and a general local touch in the vocabulary of the web page not just mere translation.

Proper Titles: Titles of the important people in the company, titles of the people in the contact information, and titles of people on the organizational charts.

Singh and Baack (2004), Singh and Matsuo (2004), Singh, Zhao and Hu (2003, 2004).

APPENDIX 3.3

The following are details of the results of the study discussed on page 62. The results indicate significant differences in depiction of cultural values across the web sites of the four countries, with local web sites depicting local cultural values. The multivariate test results of MANOVA show that country main effect is highly significant with a Wilks lambda of .019 (F = 31.96, p < .000). Prior to conducting post-hoc tests, the data were subjected to homogeneity of variance test and the assumption was satisfied. The test of between-subject effects and the post-hoc Tukey test (see Table 3.5) reveal that most local web sites depict cultural values consistent with their national culture (Singh, Zhao, and Hu 2004).

TABLE 3.5   MANOVA Results (F-Values) on Cultural Values

	Main effects[a]		Interactions[a]	Tukey test[b]
Values	Country (C)	Industry (I)	C × I	Group comparisons[c]
Collectivism	11.00**	ns	4.81**	Jp>In&US; Ch>US
Individualism	137.12**	4.75*	ns	US>Jp,In&Ch; Jp&In>Ch
Uncertainty Avoidance	7.58**	ns	ns	In>US&Jp
Power Distance	25.81**	ns	ns	In,Jp&Ch>US
Masculinity	6.70**	ns	5.51**	Jp&In>US
High Context	114.19**	4.21*	3.61*	Jp>US,In&Ch;Ch>US&In
Low Context	29.00**	ns	ns	US>Jp&Ch; In>Jp&Ch

[a]F-Values
[b]Comparisons that are significant at <.05 level are reported.
[c]Jp = Japan; In = India; Ch = China; US = United States
*p < .05; **p < .01
Adapted from Singh, Zhao, and Hu (2004).

REFERENCES

Albers-Miller, N.D. and Gelb, B.D. (1996) Business Advertising Appeals as Mirror of Cultural Dimensions: A Study of Eleven Countries, *Journal of Advertising*, 25(Winter), 57–70.

Borden, G.A. (1991) *Cultural Orientation: An Approach to Understanding Intercultural Communication*. Englewood Cliffs, NJ: Prentice Hall.

Cheng, H. and Schweitzer, J.C. (1996) Cultural Values Reflected in Chinese and U.S Television Commercials, *Journal of Advertising Research*, 36(3) (May/June), 27–45.

Cho, B., Kwon, U., Gentry, J.W., Jun, S., and Kropp, F., (1999) Cultural Values Reflected in Theme and Execution: A Comparative Study of U.S. and Korean Television. *Journal of Advertising*, 28 (4), 59–73.

Clark, T. (1990) International Marketing and National Character: A Review and Proposal for an Integrative Theory, *Journal of Marketing*, 54(Oct), 66–79.

Cutler, B.D. and Javalgi, R.S.G. (1992) A Cross-Cultural Analysis of Visual Components of Print Advertising: The United States and European Community, *Journal of Advertising Research*, 32(Jan/Feb), 71–80.

Feather, N. (1990) Bridging the Gap between Values and Action. In E. Higgins and R. Sorrentino (eds.), *Handbook of Motivation and Cognition*, Vol. 12. New York: Guilford.

Feather, N. (1995) Values, Valences, and Choice, *Journal of Personality and Social Psychology*, 68, 1135–1151.

Fock, H. (2000) Cultural Influences on Marketing Communication on the World Wide Web, *Paper Presented at the Multicultural Marketing Conference*, Hong Kong, Sept.

Gregory, G.D. and Munch, J.M. (1997) Cultural Values in International Advertising: An Example of Familial Norms and Roles in Mexico, *Psychology & Marketing*, 14(2), 99–119.

Gudykunst, W.B. (1998) *Bridging Differences: Effective Intergroup Communication*, 3rd ed. Thousand Oaks, CA: Sage Publications.

Hall, E.T. (1976) Beyond Culture. Garden City, NY: Doubleday.

Hall, E.T. and Hall, M.R. (1990) *Understanding Cultural Differences*. Yarmouth, ME: Intercultural Press.

Hofstede, G. (1980) *Culture's Consequences: International Differences in Work-Related Values*. Beverly Hills, CA: Sage Publications.

Hofstede, G. (1991) *Culture and Organizations: Software of the Mind*. London: McGraw-Hill.

Huang, J.H. (1995) Cultural Values as Manifested in U.S. and Taiwan Television Advertising. In B.B. Stern and G.M. Zinkhan (eds.), *Proceedings, AMA Educators Conference*, 155–160. Washington, D.C. Chicago: American Marketing Association.

Inkeles, A. and Levinson, D.J. (1969) National Character: The Study of Modal Personality and Sociocultural Systems. In G. Lindzey and E. Aronson (eds.), *The Handbook of Social Psychology*, Vol. 4. Reading, MA: Addison-Wesley.

Kluckhohn, F.R and Strodtbeck, F.Z. (1961) *Variations in Value Orientations*. Westport, CT: Greenwood Press.

Marketing News (2004) To Win Latino Market, Know Pitfalls, Learn Rewards, March 1, 14, 19.

McCarty, J.A. and Hattwick, P.M. (1992) Cultural Value Orientations: A Comparison of Magazines Advertisement from United States and Mexico, *Advances in Consumer Research*, 19, 34–38.

Mooij, M de (1998) *Global Marketing and Advertising, Understanding Cultural Paradoxes*. U.K: Sage Publications

Mooij, M. de (2000) The Future Is Predictable for International Marketers, *International Marketing Review*, 17(2), 103–113.

Mueller, B. (1987) Reflections of Culture: An Analysis of Japanese and American Advertising Appeals, *Journal of Advertising Research*, 27(3), 51–59.

Ogden, D.T., Ogden, J.R., and Schau, H.J. (2004) Exploring the Impact of Culture and Acculturation on Consumer Purchase Decisions: Towards a Multicultural Perspective, Academy of Marketing Science Review, (03), Online www.amsreview.org/articles/ogden02-2004.pdf.

Parsons, T. and Shils, E.A. (1951) Toward a General Theory of Action. Cambridge, MA: Harvard University Press.

Pollay, R.W. (1983) Measuring the Cultural Values Manifest in Advertising. In J.H. Leigh and C.R. Martin (eds.), Current Issues and Research in Advertising, 72–92. Ann Arbor: MI: University of Michigan Press.

Simon, S.J. (1999) A Cross Cultural Analysis of Web Site Design: An Empirical Study of Global Web Users, *Paper Presented at the Seventh Cross-Cultural Consumer and Business Studies Research Conference*, Cancun, Mexico.

Singh, N. and Baack, W. D. (2004) Studying Cultural Values on the Web: A Cross-Cultural Study of U.S. and Mexican Web Sites, *Journal of Computer Mediated Communication*, 9(4), *www.ascusc.org/jcmc/vol9/issue4/*

Singh, N. and Matsuo, H. (2004) Measuring Cultural Adaptation on the Web: A Study of U.S. and Japanese Websites, *Journal of Business Research*, 57(8), 864–872.

Singh, N., Zhao, H., and Hu, X. (2003) Cultural Adaptation on the Web: A Study of American Companies' Domestic and Chinese Web Sites, *Journal of Global Information Management*, 11(3), 63–81.

Singh, N., Zhao, H., and Hu, X. (2004) Analyzing the Cultural Content of Web Sites: A Cross-National Comparison of China, India, Japan, and U.S., *International Marketing Review*, 69–88.

Tansey, R., Hyman, M.R., and Zinkhan, G.M. (1990) Cultural Themes in Brazilian and U.S Auto Ads: A Cross-Cultural Comparison, *Journal of Advertising*, 19(2), 30–39.

Thomas, G., Hult, M., Kandemir, D., and Keillor, B. (2004) A Study of the Service Encounter in Eight Countries, *Journal of International Marketing*, 12(1), 9–35).

Triandis, H.C. (1972) *The Analysis of Subjective Culture*. New York: John Wiley.

Triandis, H.C. (1982) Review of Culture's Consequences: International Differences in Work-Related Values, *Human Organization*, 41, 86–90.

Triandis, H.C. (1994) *Culture and Social Behavior*. New York: McGraw-Hill.

Trompenaars, F. (1994) *Riding the Waves of Culture: Understanding Diversity in Global Business*. New York: Irwin Professional Publishing.

Tse, D.K., Belk, R.W., and Zhou, N. (1989) Becoming a Consumer Society: A Longitudinal and Cross-Cultural Content Analysis of Print Ads from Hong Kong, The People's Republic of China, and Taiwan, *Journal of Consumer Research*, 15(March), 457–472.

Zandpour, F. and (A Team of 10 Researchers) (1994) Global Reach and Local Touch: Achieving Cultural Fitness in TV Advertising, *Journal of Advertising Research*, 34(5), 35–63.

4

CULTURAL CUSTOMIZATION: INDIVIDUALISM-COLLECTIVISM

This chapter focuses on the cultural value of individualism-collectivism *and provides guidelines for designing web sites that conform to this value.*

CHAPTER HIGHLIGHTS

INDIVIDUALISM-COLLECTIVISM: IN BRIEF

Key Issue

A belief in the importance of the goals of the individual (individualism) versus the goals of the group (collectivism).

Countries High on Individualism

United States, Australia, United Kingdom, the Netherlands, Canada, and New Zealand (see page 73 for a comprehensive list of country scores).

Countries High on Collectivism

Guatemala, Ecuador, Panama, Venezuela, Colombia, and Indonesia (see page 73 for a comprehensive list of country scores).

Operationalizing Collectivism on the Web

Community Relations: A community policy, giving back to community, social responsibility policy.

Clubs/Chat Rooms: Member clubs, product-based clubs, chat with company people, chat with interest groups, message boards, discussion groups, and live talks.

Newsletter: Online subscriptions, magazines, and newsletters.

Family Theme: Pictures of family, pictures of teams of employees, mention of employee teams and emphasis on team and collective work responsibility in vision statement or elsewhere on the web site, and emphasis on customers as a family.

Symbols and Pictures of National Identity: Flags, pictures of historic monuments, pictures reflecting uniqueness of the country, country-specific symbols in the form of icons, and indexes.

Loyalty Programs: Customer loyalty programs, company credit cards for specific country, and special membership programs.

Links to Local Web Sites: Links to local partners, related country-specific companies, and other local web sites from a particular country.

Operationalizing Individualism on the Web

Good Privacy Statement: Privacy policy and how personal information will be protected or used.

Independence Theme: Images and themes depicting self-reliance, self-recognition, and achievement.

Product Uniqueness: Unique selling points of the product and product differentiation features.

Personalization: Gift recommendations, individual acknowledgments or greeting, and web page personalization.

Caveats

1. The cultural value of individualism-collectivism is one of the five values in the Cultural Values Framework that addresses the "*behavioral*" component of culture. Each country is a unique blend of all of the relevant cultural values; as such, for true cultural customization, all relevant values must be included. Further, the other two components of culture, *perception* and *symbolism* (discussed in Chapter 2), must also be part of any attempt at cultural customization of a web site. The features listed here are based on Singh, Zhao, and Hu (2003) and Singh and Matsuo (2004).

2. The above features, when emphasized in a web site, make the site more closely customized to the cultural value of individualism or collectivism. It should be noted that such features might well be present in sites that are not attempting such customization; however, it is not the mere presence of these features that matters, but the degree to which they are emphasized in a web site.

INDIVIDUALISM-COLLECTIVISM: COUNTRY SCORES

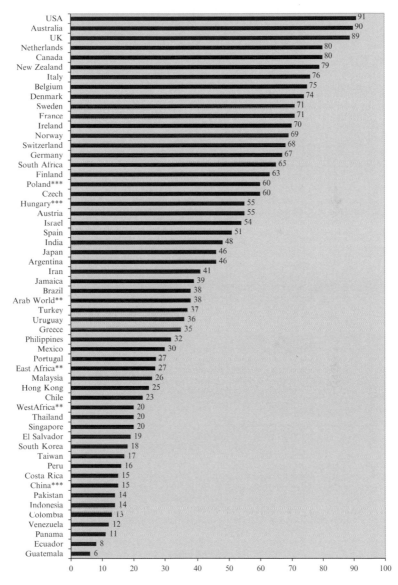

*** Estimated values
** *Arab World:* Egypt, Iraq, Kuwait Lebanon, Libya, Saudi Arabia, United Arab Emirates.
** *East Africa:* Ethiopia, Kenya, Tanzania, Zambia
** *West Africa:* Ghana, Nigeria, Sierra Leone

Source: Hofstede, G., *"Culture's Consequences: Comparing Values, Behaviors, Institutions, and Organizations,"* Sage Publications, 2001

FIGURE 4.1   Individualism-Collectivism: Country Scores, Descending Order (Higher scores signify Individualism).

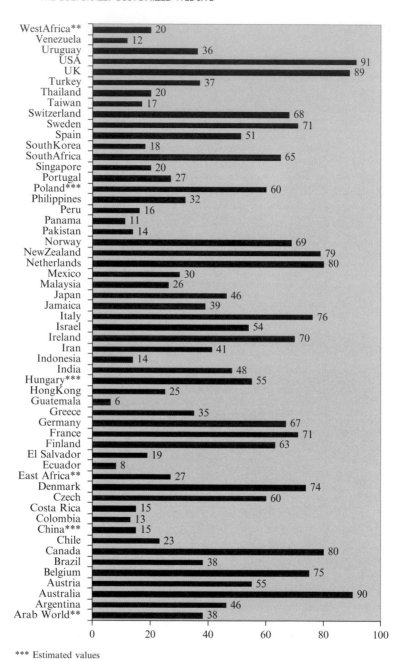

*** Estimated values

FIGURE 4.2   Individualism-Collectivism: Country Scores, Alphabetized Order (Higher scores signify Individualism).

RESEARCH ON INDIVIDUALISM-COLLECTIVISM

The bi-polar individualism-collectivism value has been widely studied in cross-cultural research (Gudykunst 1998; Hofstede 1980, 1991, Triandis 1982). This cultural dimension focuses on an individual's relationship with society or other individuals. In individualist societies, ties between individuals are loose, personal freedom is valued, and individual decision-making is encouraged. Individualist cultures encourage personal achievement, and the population in general is more self-reliant. Identity in individualist cultures is centered on "I-consciousness"; therefore, people in individualist cultures value self-reliance, achievement, independence, and freedom (Gudykunst 1998; Hofstede 1980).

Highly individualistic countries include the United States, Australia, Canada, the United Kingdom, the Netherlands, New Zealand, and Italy. Hofstede's conclusions on these countries are further validated by research that indicates advertising in such cultures emphasizes the independence theme in the form of individual determinism, independence, competition, autonomy, and non-conformity (Albers-Miller and Gelb 1996; Cho et al. 1999; Cheng and Schweitzer 1996; Mueller 1987; Zandpour et al. 1994).

High collectivist countries include Guatemala, Ecuador, Panama, Venezuela, Colombia, Indonesia, Pakistan, and China. In collectivist societies, individuals are connected with strong societal bonds, group well-being takes precedence over individual well-being, and there is emphasis on group decision-making and conformity. For example, research indicates that in collectivist societies such as China, people are willing to sacrifice themselves for the greater benefit of the social unit or the society (Yau 1988). Furthermore, collectivist societies emphasize in-group obligations, extended family structures, interdependence (Cho et al. 1999; Han and Shavitt 1994), and preserving the welfare of others (Gudykunst 1998). Societal norms and societal pressure have been shown to have a significant impact on behavioral intention formation in collectivist societies (Lee and Green 1991). Research on advertising in such countries shows advertising to be congruent to their cultural identity, with an emphasis on group-consensus appeals, family security, and family ties (Han and Shavitt 1994; Lin 2001).

DESIGNING WEB SITES FOR COLLECTIVISM

When designing web sites for collectivist cultures, it is important to emphasize collectivist values (Singh and Baack, 2004; Singh and Matsuo, 2004; Singh, Zhao, and Hu 2003). Based on the literature and our own survey and content analysis of communication content of various cultures (see Chapter 3), we recommend that companies need to highlight the following features when designing web sites for collectivist cultures (Singh and Baack 2004; Singh and Matsuo 2004; Singh, Zhao, and Hu 2003):

Clubs/Chat Rooms

In collectivist societies, there is an emotional dependence of individuals on organizations and society (Hofstede 1980); thus, people need forums, places, or clubs where they can share their concerns, views, and emotions and develop relationships. Xi'an International University of China prominently shows its core values or advantages on its home page, and one of them is highlighted as "social skills development." The collectivist orientation leads to an increased use of informal channels of communication. For example, the Chinese tend to rely more on word-of-mouth communication to seek market information (Yau 1988). Moreover, people in collectivist cultures see themselves in relation to specific groups or institutions. Pollay (1983) emphasizes the nurturance theme, wherein members of a group provide each other with support and sympathy. It is the product that brings the product users together; thus, product-based clubs can serve as arenas to facilitate sharing of opinions and an informal source of market and product information (Singh and Matsuo 2004; Singh, Zhao, and Hu 2004). For example, the Japanese web sites of Fujitsu and Olympus prominently depict features like camera clubs and news clubs. The Chinese web site of Olympus (*www.olympus.com.cn/club/index.asp*) also prominently features a photo club that encourages membership and sharing of information (Figure 4.3). Similarly, *www.banateen.com*, an Arabic web site, has a whole section devoted to chat, clubs, and online forums (Figures 4.4, 4.5). Thus, companies can incorporate theme-based chat rooms, member clubs, product-based clubs or discussion areas, and similar features that enhance online sharing and online community development.

FIGURE 4.3   *www.olympus.com*

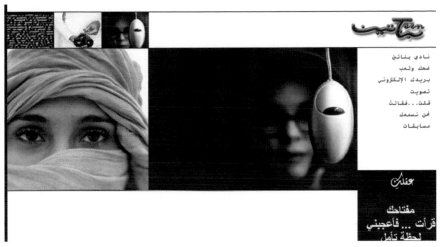

FIGURE 4.4 *www.banateen.com*

FIGURE 4.5 *www.banateen.com*

Community Relations

Collectivist societies place emphasis on community-based social order (Hofstede 1991) and people give precedence to societal needs over individual needs (Yau 1988), Furthermore, collectivist societies emphasize in-group obligations, interdependence, and preserving the welfare of others. Societal norms and societal pressure have been shown to have a significant impact on behavioral intention formation in collectivist societies (Lee and Green 1991).

Advertising in collectivist societies has been shown to emphasize appeals relating to interdependent relationships. For example, Chinese advertisements have been found to emphasize group-consensus appeals (Lin 2001). Thus, emphasizing the community relationships on web sites would help companies show their concern for the society and would reflect the interdependence theme. For example, Jaring, a Malaysian Internet service provider has a unique section on "Jaring Lend a Hand," which is a free service by the company to help locate lost items and missing persons through public awareness and cooperation (Figures 4.6, 4.7). Companies targeting collectivist societies can incorporate information on their role in local community, unique local community initiatives, corporate philanthropy subsections, social responsibility policy, and any other information that affirms local community investment (Singh and Baack 2004; Singh and Matsuo 2004 Singh, Zhao, and Hu 2003).

Family Theme

Collectivist cultures are more likely to emphasize in-group obligations, family security, and family ties (Han and Shavitt 1994; Zahedi et al. 2001). In collectivist cultures, the "we theme" and the depiction of family integrity or "family" in a positive manner in advertising is common. In such cultures, family orientation extends beyond the immediate family and encompasses close friends, work colleagues, and business partners. Family is seen as the source of identity in collectivist culture, and it gets reflected in the plethora of extended family ties and extensive vocabulary distinguishing various interpersonal bonds that are unique to such family orientation (Singh, Zhao, and Hu 2004).

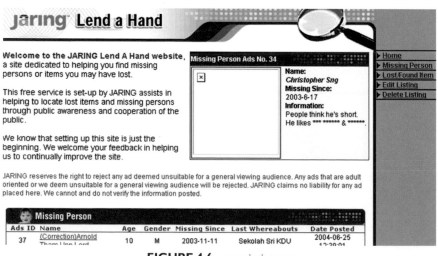

FIGURE 4.6 *www.jaring.com*

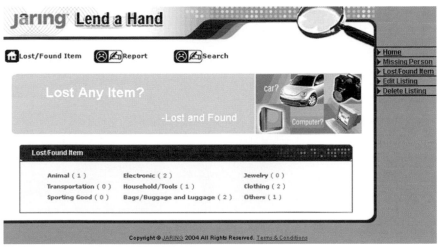

FIGURE 4.7   *www.jaring.com*

For example, in China and India, familial bonds are reflected in complex family terminology wherein there are separate, unique words for older brother, younger brother, older sister, younger sister, and maternal and paternal uncles and aunts. Thus, emphasizing the family theme in the form of pictures, themes, and web content would help connect with the family-orientation aspect of collectivist cultures (Figures 4.8, 4.9). Pictures and themes showing family bonding, family enjoyment, teamwork, togetherness, employees as

FIGURE 4.8   *www.dico.com*

FIGURE 4.9   *www.dico.com*

family, friendship, and family occasions can effectively communicate the importance of family in collectivist cultures (Singh and Baack, 2004; Singh and Matsuo, 2004; Singh, Zhao, and Hu 2003).

Loyalty Programs

Building lasting relationships and engendering a sense of loyalty are important to people in collectivist cultures (Trompenaars 1994). For example, Chinese consumers tend to be more brand-loyal than their counterparts in the West. They conform to group norms and therefore tend to purchase the same brand that other members of the group recommend. Moreover, policies and procedures based on loyalty, conformity, and orderliness are valued in collectivist societies (Hofstede 1980). For example, Japanese people value the feeling of *amae*, which means looking out for others in the group and loyalty to the group. Thus, having features on the web site that engender loyalty can help tune the web sites to the collectivist orientation. Loyalty to company, brand, and products can be depicted in the form of country-specific credit card based loyalty points programs, exclusive customer clubs for the local country consumers, frequent web shopping points programs, and so forth (Singh and Baack 2004; Singh and Matsuo 2004; Singh, Zhao, and Hu 2003).

Newsletter

In collectivist societies, people value group membership, group involvement, and a sense of belongingness (Hofstede 1980). Such cultures emphasize the goals, needs, and views of the in-group (Gudykunst 1998), which leads to more in-group (within-country) orientation and patriotism. Thus, the identity of people in collectivist cultures is based on the country's social system; as such, providing visitors to a web site with country-specific news helps people identify themselves with their society. Moreover, newsletters serve as a vehicle for engendering affiliation and membership with the company. Newsletters help keep the customers in the loop of what is going on in the company, in terms of new products, changes, offers, and updates. Newsletters designed specifically for the local culture, with news, reviews, and comments pertaining to the local country, can serve as a good strategy for foreign firms to show local affiliation and local commitment. Several collectivist societies like Japan, China, Malaysia, and countries in the Middle East prominently show newsletters and link to them from their home pages. Examples include the local newsletter on *www.Arabiawide.com* (an Arabic search engine), Olympus Techno Zone magazine section at the Olympus web site (Japanese) *www.olympus.co.jp/jp/magazine/techzone/*, and an Internet magazine by Jaring (*www.magazine.jaring.my/2004/june/*) (Figures 4.10–4.13). Thus, newsletters can be depicted in the form of web-based magazines, local news and reviews, product-based newsletters, online subscriptions, and similar features.

Links to Local Web Sites

In collectivist societies, people invest a lot in relationship capital. Having links to local web sites shows that the company is well connected within the country

FIGURE 4.10   *www.jaring.com*

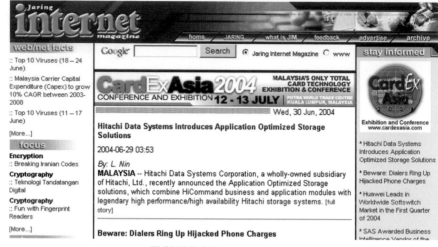

FIGURE 4.11   *www.jaring.com*

FIGURE 4.12   *www.olympus.com*

and has legitimate relationships with local companies. For example, doing business in China requires *guanxi* or social contacts; similarly, in Japan many argue the foundation for the existence of *keiretsu* is the collectivist nature of its culture. Links to local companies are also perceived as evidence that a particular company is well established in the country and can be trusted. This is particularly important in collectivist societies that have a clear *in-group* and *out-group* orientation (in-group stands for members belonging to one's

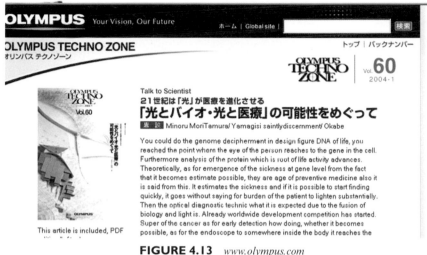

FIGURE 4.13   *www.olympus.com*

nationality, race, ethnicity or group; out-group stands for anybody who is not a member of such a group and thus does not share a common sense of group identification.) To be perceived as a part of an in-group, companies need to tap into relationship capital, invest in local partners and contacts, and prominently depict this on their web sites. Even local companies in collectivist cultures proudly depict their local connections via such links (Singh, Zhao, and Hu 2004). For example, Olympus and Fujitsu web sites for the Japanese audience show several local links to local web sites such as racquetball associations, travel agencies, and tours for viewing cherry blossoms. Similarly, the Indian web site that sells scooters and motorbikes (*www.premjis.com*) has several links to special interest local scooter or bike web sites like *www.india-bike.com, www.motorcyclecity.com*, and so forth (Figures 4.14–4.16). Links to domestic locations can be in the form of links to local partners, related country-specific companies, and other local, special interest web sites such as weather, local news, local events, and so on (Singh and Baack 2004; Singh and Matsuo 2004; Singh, Zhao, and Hu 2003).

Symbols and Pictures of National Identity

Collectivist societies emphasize identity based on social systems (Hofstede 1980) and historical traditions. Studies by Cheng and Schweitzer (1996) and Zandpour et al. (1994) show that advertisements in collectivist societies depict the use of symbols and pictures of national identity. Moreover, in-group consciousness is manifested in the material world through symbols, icons, and pictures emphasizing national pride, national heritage, local

allibhai premji tyrewalla

Home What's New Finance Spares Helmets Used Bikes Exports Tourism

The classic Royal Enfield Bullet motorcycle is your chance to ride a piece of motorcycling history. Explore the complete range of Royal Enfield motorcycles, spare parts and accessories from one of India's most experienced motorcycle dealers.

Autorickshaws, mopeds, motorcycles and scooters from Bajaj Auto, Hero Honda, Kinetic, LML, TVS Motor Company (formerly TVS Suzuki) and Yamaha are also available at our multi-franchise dealership.

FIGURE 4.14 *www.premjis.com*

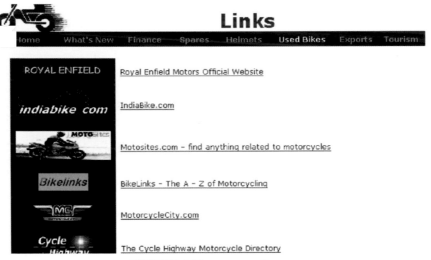

FIGURE 4.15 *www.premjis.com*

architectural achievements, local history, local role models, and other depictions of national identity. It is also important to use local models and local celebrities to endorse or sell products. Advertising literature indicates that ethnic or national models are more effective than foreign models. For example, see the Mexican web site, *www.cacto.com/methodologia.html* shown in Figure 4.17.

Biker's Shack

A NEW Bikers site built by Bikers for Bikers
Drop into the Shack again to see what's changed!

TOURISM LINKS

Wheel of India

Motorcycle Tours through India on Royal Enfield Motorcycles

India Overland Great site for those planning overland road trips in India. Tips on where to stay and what to see.

Road Maps for India, all its states and cities.

FIGURE 4.16 *www.premjis.com*

FIGURE 4.17 *www.cacto.com*

DESIGNING WEB SITES FOR INDIVIDUALISM

In individualist cultures, people value individual freedom and expression. The Web has penetrated most extensively in Western individualist nations like the United States, Canada, United Kingdom, and other European countries; as such, at the present time, the Web is, to a large extent, impregnated with individualist values like individual personalization, emphasis on personal privacy, and highlighting product uniqueness. In the following paragraphs, we elaborate the reasons to emphasize certain individualistic features and tips to incorporate them (Singh and Baack 2004; Singh and Matsuo 2004; Singh, Zhao, and Hu 2003).

Independence Theme

Social identity in individualist cultures is centered around "I-consciousness"; therefore, the independence theme is common among such cultures (Lin 2001). People in individualist cultures value self-reliance, achievement, independence, and freedom (Hofstede 1980). Advertising in individualist cultures has been shown to emphasize the independence theme in the form of individual determinism, independence, competition, autonomy, and non-conformity (Albers-Miller and Gelb 1996; Cheng and Schweitzer, 1996; Cho et al. 1999; Mueller 1987; Zandpour et al. 1994). For example, the U.S. web site of Pontiac Aztec highlights independence as a part of brand image. The Charles Schwab web site underscores the independence theme with statements like, "Invest on your terms," "Now the choice is yours" (Figure 4.18).

A Good Privacy Statement

In individualist cultures, because personal identity is important, so is its protection. People are hesitant to share personal information with strangers and reserve personal conversations with close friends or family. In stark contrast,

FIGURE 4.18   *www.charlesschwab.com*

in countries such as China and India and in the Middle East, people are more prone to sharing personal information with colleagues, friends, and even strangers. Most web sites in the United States, United Kingdom, Canada, and Australia have a clear privacy policy. Usually the link to the privacy policy is found at the bottom of the home page. Some examples include web sites of several major online companies like MSN, Yahoo, and Amazon. Although a privacy policy is seen as near universal on Western web sites, various collectivist country web sites are not big on privacy policy. For example, a study by Forrester Research found that several Japanese web sites do not provide a clear privacy policy (Rogowski, Temkin, and Amato 2003). The web site of *www.Monster.com* highlights the importance of its privacy policy right at the top of the home page (Figure 4.19).

Personalization and Product Uniqueness

Individualism translates into emphasis on "standing out from the crowd," non-conformity, and uniqueness (Albers-Miller and Gelb 1996; Mueller 1987, 1992). Thus, promotional appeals in such cultures should be directed toward individuals, and the message should be addressed to and made relevant to an individual (Kale 1991). People in such cultures value products that help them become self-reliant, distinctive, independent, and are responsive to their individual needs. Commercials in individualist cultures frequently depict appeals relating to uniqueness, originality, variety, reliability, and distinctiveness (Albers-Miller and Gelb 1996; Cheng and Schweitzer 1996; Mueller 1987, 1992; Zandpour et al. 1994). Thus, web strategies should emphasize unique

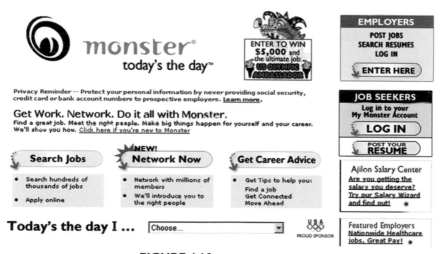

FIGURE 4.19   *www.monster.com*

selling points of the product, product differentiation features, features like gift recommendations, suggestions box, individual acknowledgments or greeting, and web page personalization. Companies need to highlight their unique selling proposition or a statement that clearly reflects the benefit statement—up front on the web site. Use of bold or distinct font may further enhance its visibility. It is also important to personalize the web site of specific web pages to individual customers. For example, several American companies personalize their web pages for customers; companies deliver personalized news, weather information, stock quotes, and product and gift recommendations. Amazon (*www.Amazon.com*) practices online personalization by virtually creating a customized Amazon store for its customers, based on customer preferences, past customer searches, customer personal data, and customer lifestyle information. Customers at *www.Amazon.com* can actually express their individuality by creating their own area called, "About you area," where they can create their profile, make recommendations, post reviews, and even invite friends to view their profile and wish lists (Figures 4.20, 4.21).

Visit www.theculturallycustomizedwebsite.com for additional information and updates.

CHAPTER KEYS

Collectivism and Individualism are the polar opposites of the same cultural value, and various countries fall on this continuum, depending on their collectivistic or individualistic tendencies.

Help > Amazon.com Services > Friends & Favorites > Your "About You" Area

Your About You Area

Friends & Favorites is a service that puts you in touch with opinions and information from people who matter to you. Just add your friends and favorite reviewers to your Favorite People list. We'll gather up reviews, recommendations, and opinions from your Favorite People and put it all right in front of you in your very own About You area.

Suggestions Given

Suggestions Given is a service that allows you to make suggestions that will help us improve our product lists. For example, if you see shoes appearing on a list on a page devoted to pants, you may want to let us know that the shoes do not belong on that page. When you see a link such as, "Are these results helpful to you? Let us know," click on it to indicate whether items in that product list do not suit the page. Clicking on the link will bring up a pop-up window; in the window, select the check boxes next to the products you feel do not belong on the page. We'll look at all the suggestions and modify our product lists to reflect your and other customers' views.

Favorite People

FIGURE 4.20   *www.amazon.com*

FIGURE 4.21   *www.amazon.com*

If the country of interest is predominantly collectivist, a web site can be adapted to conform to this value by incorporating the following: community relations, clubs/chat rooms, newsletter, family themes, symbols and pictures of national identity, loyalty programs, and links to local web sites.

If the country of interest is predominantly individualistic, the following can be incorporated into a web site: Good privacy statement, independence theme, product uniqueness, and personalized features.

EXERCISES

Students

Find two individuals from a collectivist culture (Latin American countries, Mexico, China, Japan), and together, visit two *local* (i.e., domestic) web sites from their countries. Keeping in mind the issues discussed in this chapter, identify how collectivist values are manifested on the web sites of the country you have chosen. Compare and contrast these local web sites with that of a multinational company targeting that particular collectivist country.

Do the same exercise with two people from an individualist culture.

Managers

Identify the web sites of leading companies in *your industry* and, using the framework provided in this chapter, see how these companies are incorporating collectivist or individualist features on web sites targeted to such countries.

Pick *other industries* that have a tradition of serving these countries, and analyze the web sites of the successful companies in those industries. Often, another industry's company web sites can be used as a "higher standard" and a more useful benchmark than the web sites of companies from your own industry.

REFERENCES

Albers-Miller, N.D. and Gelb, B.D. (1996) Business Advertising Appeals as Mirror of Cultural Dimensions: A Study of Eleven Countries, *Journal of Advertising*, 25(Winter), 57–70.

Cheng, H. and Schweitzer, J.C. (1996) Cultural Values Reflected in Chinese and U.S. Television Commercials, *Journal of Advertising Research*, 36(3) (May/June), 27–45.

Cho, B., Kwon, U., Gentry, J.W., Jun, S., Kropp, F. (1999) Cultural Values Reflected in Theme and Execution: A Comparative Study of U.S. and Korean Television. *Journal of Advertising*, 28 (4), 59–73.

Gudykunst, W.B. (1998) Bridging differences: *Effective Intergroup Communication*, 3rd ed. Thousand Oaks, CA: Sage Publications.

Han, S.-P. and Shavitt, S. (1994) Persuasion and Culture: Advertising Appeals in Individualistic and Collectivistic Societies, *Journal of Experimental Social Psychology*, 30(July), 8–18.

Hofstede, G. (1980) *Culture's Consequences: International Differences in Work-Related Values*. Beverly Hills, CA: Sage Publications.

Hofstede, G. (1991) *Culture and Organizations: Software of the Mind*. London: McGraw-Hill.

Kale, H. S. (1991) Culture-Specific Marketing Communications: An Analytical Approach, *International Marketing Review*, 8 (2), 18–30.

Lee, C. and Green, R.T. (1991) Cross-Cultural Examination of the Fishbein Behavioral Intentions Model, *Journal of International Business Studies*, 22(2), 289–305.

Lin, C.A. (2001) Cultural Values Reflected in Chinese and American Television Advertising, *Journal of Advertising*, 30(4), 83–94.

Mueller, B. (1987) Reflections of Culture: An Analysis of Japanese and American Advertising Appeals, *Journal of Advertising Research*, 27(3) (June/July), 51–59.

Pollay, R.W. (1983) Measuring the Cultural Values Manifest in Advertising. In J.H. Leigh and C.R. Martin (eds.), *Current Issues and Research in Advertising,* 72–92. Ann Arbor: MI: University of Michigan Press.

Rogowski, R., Temkin, B.D., and Amato, M. (2003) How Effective Are Japanese Web Sites, A Report from Forrester Research-*www.forrester.com*

Singh, N. and Baack, W. D. (2004) Studying Cultural Values on the Web: A Cross-Cultural Study of U.S. and Mexican Web Sites, *Journal of Computer Mediated Communication,* 9(4), *www.ascusc.org/jcmc/vol9/issue4/*

Singh, N. and Matsuo, H. (2004) Measuring Cultural Adaptation on the Web: A Study of U.S. and Japanese Websites, *Journal of Business Research*, 57(8), 864–872.

Singh, N., Zhao, H. and Hu, X. (2003) Cultural Adaptation on the Web: A Study of American Companies' Domestic and Chinese Web Sites, *Journal of Global Information Management*, 11(3), 63–81.

Singh, N., Zhao, H., and Hu, X. (2004) Analyzing the Cultural Content of Web Sites: A Cross-National Comparison of China, India, Japan, and U.S., *International Marketing Review*, in press.

Triandis, H.C. (1982) Review of Culture's Consequences: International Differences in Work-Related Values, *Human Organization*, 41, 86–90.

Trompenaars, F. (1994) *Riding the Waves of Culture: Understanding Diversity in Global Business.* New York: Irwin Professional Publishing.

Yau, H.M.O. (1988) Chinese Cultural Values Their Dimensions and Marketing Implications, *European Journal of Marketing*, 22(5), 44–57.

Zandpour, F., and (A Team of 10 Researchers) (1994) Global Reach and Local Touch: Achieving Cultural Fitness in TV Advertising, *Journal of Advertising Research*, 34(5), 35–63.

Zahedi, F., Van Pelt, W.V., and Sont, J. (2001) A Conceptual Framework for International Web Design, IEEE Transactions on Professional Communication, 44(2), 83–103.

5

CULTURAL CUSTOMIZATION: UNCERTAINTY AVOIDANCE

This chapter focuses on the cultural value of uncertainty avoidance *and provides guidelines for designing web sites that conform to this value.*

CHAPTER HIGHLIGHTS

UNCERTAINTY AVOIDANCE: IN BRIEF
UNCERTAINTY AVOIDANCE: COUNTRY SCORES
RESEARCH ON UNCERTAINTY AVOIDANCE
DESIGNING WEB SITES FOR UNCERTAINTY AVOIDANCE

UNCERTAINTY AVOIDANCE: IN BRIEF

Key Issue

The importance of predictability, structure, and order (high uncertainty avoidance) versus willingness for risk-taking, less structure, and ambiguity (low uncertainty avoidance).

Countries High on Uncertainty Avoidance

Greece, Portugal, Guatemala, Uruguay, El Salvador, Belgium, and Japan (see page 95 for a comprehensive list of country scores).

Countries Low on Uncertainty Avoidance

Singapore, Jamaica, Denmark, Hong Kong, Sweden, Ireland, and the United Kingdom (see page 95 for a comprehensive list of country scores).

Operationalizing Uncertainty Avoidance on the Web

Customer Service: FAQs, customer service options, customer help, customer contact, or customer service e-mails.

Guided Navigation: Site maps, well-displayed links, links in the form of pictures or buttons, forward, backward, up and down navigation buttons.

Tradition Theme: Emphasis on history and ties of a particular company with a nation, emphasis on respect, veneration of elderly and the culture, phrases like "most respected company," "keeping the tradition alive," "for generations," "company legacy."

Local Stores: Mention of contact information for local offices, dealers, and shops.

Local Terminology: Use of country-specific metaphors, names of festivals, puns, and a general local touch in the vocabulary of the web page, not just mere translation.

Free Trials or Downloads: Free stuff, free downloads, free screen savers, free product trials, free coupons to try the products or services, free memberships, or free service information.

Toll Free Numbers: Telephone access around the clock.

Transaction Security and Testimonials: Testimonials from customers, trust-enhancing features like reliability seals, seals of trust, and ethical business practices from third parties.

Caveats

1. The cultural value of uncertainty-avoidance is one of the five values in the Cultural Values Framework that addresses the "*behavioral*" component of culture. Each country is a unique blend of all of the relevant cultural values; as such, for true cultural customization, all relevant values must be included. Further, the other two components of culture, *perception* and *symbolism* (discussed in Chapter 2), must also be part of any attempt at cultural customization of a web site. The listed features have been scientifically derived and validated (Singh and Baack 2004; Singh and Matsuo 2004; Singh, Zhao, and Hu 2003.

2. The higher the score a country has on uncertainty avoidance, the more relevant and important the web site features mentioned in the previous section become. For those countries at the low end of uncertainty avoidance, the web site characteristics are not priorities; instead for these countries, the focus should be on those values (be they collectivism-individualism, power distance, masculinity-femininity, or high-low context) on which they have high scores.

3. The above features, when emphasized in a web site, make the site more closely customized to the cultural value of uncertainty avoidance. It should be noted that such features might well be present in sites that are not attempting such customization; however, it is not the mere presence of these features that matters, but the degree to which they are emphasized in a web site.

UNCERTAINTY AVOIDANCE: COUNTRY SCORES

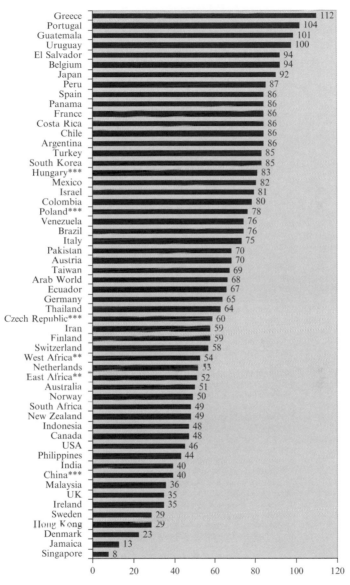

*** Estimated values
** *Arab World:* Egypt, Iraq, Kuwait Lebanon, Libya, Saudi Arabia, United Arab Emirates.
** *East Africa:* Ethiopia, Kenya, Tanzania, Zambia
** *West Africa:* Ghana, Nigeria, Sierra Leone

Source: Hofstede, G., *"Culture's Consequences: Comparing Values, Behaviors, Institutions, and Organizations,"* Sage Publications, 2001.

FIGURE 5.1   Uncertainty Avoidance: Country Scores, Descending Order (High scores signify high uncertainty avoidance).

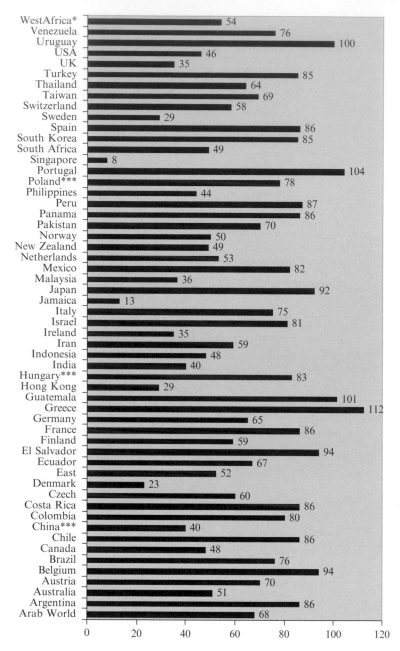

*** Estimated values
** *Arab World:* Egypt, Iraq, Kuwait Lebanon, Libya, Saudi Arabia, United Arab Emirates.
** *East Africa:* Ethiopia, Kenya, Tanzania, Zambia
** *West Africa:* Ghana, Nigeria, Sierra Leone

Source: Hofstede, G., *"Culture's Consequences: Comparing Values, Behaviors, Institutions, and Organizations,"* Sage Publications, 2001.

FIGURE 5.2 Uncertainty Avoidance: Country Scores, Alphabetized Order (High scores signify high uncertainty avoidance).

RESEARCH ON UNCERTAINTY AVOIDANCE

The uncertainty avoidance dimension proposed by Hofstede (1980) measures the extent to which cultures can deal with uncertainty and ambiguity. While uncertainty is an integral part of our lives, individuals differ in their attitudes and their responses to it. Cultures that have low tolerance for uncertainty (high uncertainty avoidance cultures) tend to be less risk takers, avoid ambiguous situations, view conflict and competition as threatening, and value security over adventure and risk (Hofstede 1980); cultures that score low on uncertainty avoidance tend to have a greater tolerance for ambiguity and risky situations. High uncertainty avoidance societies are also known to be "tight societies" that value conservatism and traditional beliefs (Hofstede 1980). Individuals from high uncertainty avoidance cultures have a need for clear rules, structure, directions, and codes of conduct. For example, Germans tend to be high on uncertainty avoidance and like to structure their lives around a set of rules (Mooij 2003). The same is true for Mexico; for example, the web site of FEMSA (Figure 5.3), a Mexican beverage company, explicitly outlines the code of conduct and what types of behaviors are expected from its employees (*www.femsa.com/templates/etica.asp*).

High uncertainty avoidance cultures also tend to use electronic media less often since this media is not well suited to reduce uncertainty (Straub et al. 1997). A study on global Internet use by Lynch, Kent, and Srinivasan (2001) found Asian online consumers to be less secure when shopping online. There could be a cultural basis for this because major Asian countries, including Japan and Taiwan, score high on uncertainty avoidance. Being a new and

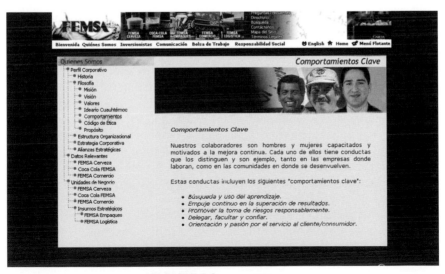

FIGURE 5.3 *www.femsa.com*

technologically sophisticated medium, the Internet has a certain degree of uncertainty associated with it, and people from high uncertainty avoidance cultures need more reassurance and uncertainty reduction features to facilitate online transactions.

DESIGNING WEB SITES FOR UNCERTAINTY AVOIDANCE

When designing web sites for uncertainty avoidance cultures, careful attention needs to be paid to site features, techniques, options, and technologies that can reduce an individual's anxiety with the medium, make it easy to follow directions and navigate, enhance transaction security, and provide extensive online and offline support. Some of the features that can help achieve this aim are discussed next, along with the underlying rationale for their inclusion (Singh and Baack 2004; Singh and Matsuo 2004; Singh, Zhao, and Hu 2003).

Customer Service

People in high uncertainty avoidance cultures value advice and help from experts in the field. For example, being high on uncertainty, Germans, through their educational system, actively try to create professionals who are experts in their area of specialization (Mooij 2003). The aim of the German education system is to produce real experts with a narrow focus in the field of expertise, unlike in American society where there are no stringent guidelines to becoming an expert. Similarly, in Japanese (high on uncertainty avoidance) society, individuals with advanced degrees, like professors, are seen as role models, and their advice is actively sought. Therefore, to make online customers from uncertainty avoidance cultures feel at ease and trusting, companies need to implement an elaborate and expert customer support department online. The online customer support should be positioned as an expert and professional service provided to help online customers. A unique way to position company people as experts in specific areas is to have personal weblogs (blogs) for each company expert. A blog is a personal diary of a person online, where he or she can post opinions, suggestions, or any form of information, and the blog is set up such that the new entries are posted on the top and older ones go to the bottom. Creating blog for company experts and having the blog link along with their bios can help position them as authority figures in their fields. An example of this at work is seen at Jupiter Research (Figure 5.4), where blogs of its research analysts are posted on the web site (*weblogs.jupiterresearch.com/analysts/sargent/*).

Another suggestion is to make the links for customer service and customer service options clearly visible on the home page of the company, so as to make it easy for customers to locate it. For example, on the Brazilian web site *www.submarino.com.br/* (Figure 5.5), you will see a customer service section

FIGURE 5.4   *www.jupiterresearch.com*

FIGURE 5.5   *www.submarino.com*

right on the front page and the security policy and payment also clearly depicted in the lower right-hand corner. (In general, on U.S. and European sites, customer service is not prominently displayed on the home page; instead, it is found typically in pages further inside the web site, and security logos tend to be at the very bottom of the home page.) Most customer service sections of web sites contain generic information about e-mail, telephone, and fax contact, or have FAQs and message boards; however, to make the sites really effective in high uncertainty avoidance cultures, the companies need to go beyond the established standards and include new and innovative ways to support online customers by including chats with product experts and technicians, live help options, videos (if broadband is available), product simulations, and other interactive features. In Japan, a country relatively high on uncertainty avoidance, customer service is important, and successful web sites provide exceptional service. For example, the web site for Japan Airlines (JAL) shows a travel support section at a prominent place on the home page. The travel support section (*www.jal.co.jp/travel/*) of JAL presents details on traveling in Japan, including weather info, world clock, maps of Japan, tourist info, flight travel made easy, hotels, renting a car, golfing, and even a video on immigration procedures to be followed (Figure 5.6). Further, the language, the graphics and pictures on this support section reflect general courtesy and respect for consumers.

Guided Navigation

Individuals in high uncertainty avoidance cultures show a preference for clear directions, instructions, and rules (Gudykunst 1998; Hofstede 1980). Thus, guided navigation becomes an important web site feature for such cultures. Features like a detailed site map, well-displayed links, links in the form of pictures or buttons, forward, backward, up and down navigation buttons, and directions on how best to browse the web site may be helpful to provide a sense

FIGURE 5.6 *www.jal.com*

of control, predictability, and ease to users from high uncertainty avoidance countries. For example, it is interesting to see that the web site of Submarino (Figure 5.7), a Brazilian company, gives their online customers step-by-step instructions on browsing and purchasing on the web site.

Another way to reduce online anxiety and enhance navigation is to have the company logo on all web pages and link them to the main home page. Thus, if visitors get lost they can click on the logo and return to the home page. This will not only assist visitors in remembering your site, but it will also give your pages a uniform look and feel. Another feature to enhance navigation is to provide a "breadcrumb trail,"– the path followed by the individual as he or she moves from web page to web page. A breadcrumb trail looks like this: Home > Section > Sub-Section > Page, and it greatly facilitates navigation. Use of different colors for visited links helps visitors know where they've been and can also enhance navigational ease. Finally, the site map must clearly show all the sections of the web site and the information contained in each of those sections. Every item in the site map must be hyperlinked to its URL. The Japan Airlines web site *www.jal.co.jp* (Figure 5.8) clearly shows the link for its site map at the top left corner.

Tradition Theme

High uncertainty avoidance societies value conservatism and traditional beliefs (Hofstede 1980). Thus, past customs and conventions are respected and qualities of the time-honored and legendary individuals are venerated

FIGURE 5.7 *www.submarino.com*

FIGURE 5.8   *www.jal.com*

(Pollay 1983). Advertising material in such cultures has been shown to depict themes like, "veneration for the elderly" and "product enjoying a long and impressive history" (Lin 2001; Mueller 1992). For example, Mexican web sites commonly use images that depict the importance of tradition (Sackmary and Scalia 1999). Thus, companies targeting high uncertainty avoidance countries can incorporate themes related to tradition; for example, the home page can reflect traditional values in the form of graphics, pictures, or statements emphasizing company traditions, company legacy, adhering to time-tested values, theme of nostalgia, "old is gold," respect for country history, national heritage, and so on. Company web sites from various countries classified as high on uncertainty avoidance commonly show the emphasis on company history, company legacy, and legacy of their founding fathers. For example, Alcatel, the French communication company, has a whole section devoted to a web page (Figure 5.9) that chronologically shows the company history since 1898 and emphasizes company legacy and its founding father (*www.alcatel.fr/apropos/histoire/index.htm*). Another French company web site that emphasizes tradition is Sodexho (*www.sodexho.com/SodexhoAnglais/detect.cfm*), which, when accessed in June 2004, showed a video clip of celebrations commemorating D-Day celebrations. Similarly, several Japanese companies like Seven Eleven, JA, Fuji, and others also emphasize the tradition theme on their web sites.

Local Stores

As high uncertainty avoidance cultures value predictability, safety, carefulness, and show low tolerance for ambiguity (Mooij 1998; Zahedi, Van Pelt,

FIGURE 5.9 *www.alcatel.fr*

and Sont 2001), depicting local store locations on web sites helps to reduce anxiety by letting people know the store locations nearest to their city. This is important also for customers in such cultures that like to browse the web for product information but would like to make the final purchase offline. For example, studies and anecdotal evidence suggests that Japanese are wary of using credit cards online and making purchases over the Web. Seven Eleven Japan addresses this issue by offering customers the option to select the products online, but pick them up and pay for them at the nearest Seven Eleven store (Figure 5.10; *www.sej.co.jp/*)

Companies can clearly show the local shop locations, dealer locations, and local office locations to help customers find offline points of contacts. Several companies have found innovative ways to communicate local store locations in the form of local maps with embedded hyperlinks to different city locations, links to sites that can give driving direction to the local stores, and more simply just a local store address and a small map. For example, Tie Break Sport, a web site from Italy (Figure 5.11) has a web page dedicated to finding locations for its local stores all over Italy (*www.tiebreak.it*). Another good example to benchmark with is McDonalds' web site from India, which has a map of India with embedded links to city locations (Figure 5.12; *www.mcdonaldsindia.com/resloc.htm*).

Local Terminology

Since high uncertainty avoidance cultures are rooted in traditions and value ritual behavior (Hofstede 1980), local metaphors, puns, and idioms are widely used. In such cultures, there is a distinct preference for local norms and conventions as a way of enhancing predictability and reducing

FIGURE 5.10   *www.sej.co.jp*

FIGURE 5.11   *www.tiebreak.it*

uncertainty (Zahedi, Van Pelt, and Sont 2001). For example, most Japanese web sites have a customary thank you note for their web visitors. The MTV web site for Japan, France, India, and other countries vividly uses local vocabulary and local metaphors. Mexican web sites also extensively use local terminology and native terms. For instance, Grupo Modelo, a brewery, uses local slogans like "*Tu tienes Corona,*" meaning "You have a crown" to

FIGURE 5.12   *www.mcdonaldsindia.com*

market their Corona brand of beer. Thus, when designing web sites for high uncertainty avoidance countries, web marketers need to emphasize local terminology, local festivals, and local visual and written metaphors to give the web sites a distinct local flavor. It might be interesting for companies targeting the Japanese market to incorporate *Haiku* or short poetic expressions to communicate company products or company philosophy *Haiku* is a revered Japanese art form. Using such intricate local touches on a web site can tell international customers that the web site is specially designed for them.

Free Trials and Downloads

People in high uncertainty avoidance cultures are less risk-taking. For them, "what is different is dangerous" (Hofstede 1991, p. 119). Thus, free trials help reduce purchase uncertainty and facilitate purchasing. It is especially easy to provide samples of products that can be digitized, like books, CDs, movies, software, and so forth. Free stuff, free downloads, free screen savers, free product trials, free coupons to try the products or services, free memberships, or free service information are some of the ways to help customers to sample things online. For example, Danone, a major French dairy and food brand, has an exclusive web area dedicated to special free offers like free magazines mailed to your doorstep, free coupons, and other offers (*www.danone.com/wps/portal/redirect/homePortal*) (Figure 5.13). Similarly, *www.7dream.com*, a Japanese e-store, also provides a variety of free material, including magazines, coupons, and so on.

FIGURE 5.13   *www.danone.com*

Transaction Security and Testimonials

Cultures high on the avoidance of uncertainty value security and low risk situations (Hofstede 1980). The Internet as a new medium that provides no face-to-face contact poses a degree of uncertainty associated with lack of physical presence. Thus, consumers from many high uncertainty avoidance countries like Germany, Belgium, Japan, Mexico, and Italy are known to be uncomfortable using their credit card or shopping online. To help reduce online anxiety and facilitate purchases and the use of online methods of payment, it is important to convince such customers of online security and build trust. One way is to have a privacy seal of trust on the web site. The most common ones found on several American sites are e-trust, TRUSTe, and Verisign. Other types of seals include reliability seals from third parties that tell customers that you follow ethical business practices (e.g., the BBBonline reliability seal in the United States). It is also important to have secure socket layer protection on the web site, security logos, a good security policy, and a detailed shipping and return policy. *Loja Americanas* is one of Brazil's largest general merchandisers; its web site explicitly states how it will protect consumers' privacy and security. They go to the extent of saying, "All the information that you supply in the process of purchasing on *www.Americanas.com* is encrypted and processed 100% by computer, without any intervention from a human being." The *www.Americanas.com* web site only uses the number of the card in the processing of the purchase and, as reported on the web site, as soon as the confirmation of the card occurs, the number is automatically destroyed and not kept in the archives of the *www.Americanas.com* (Figure 5.14).

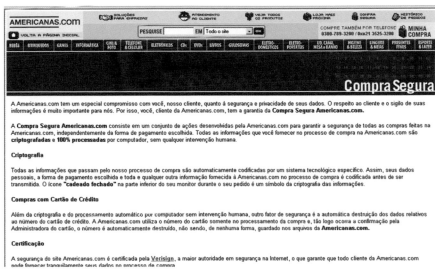

FIGURE 5.14   *www.americanas.com*

Once customers place an order on a secure site, it is important to let the customers know that their personal information will be secure and the customer order has gone through along with a confirmation number. Even when the customer registers, he or she should get a confirmation number instantly and via an e-mail for their record. Over and above these security-enhancing features, companies can post customer testimonials to make their claims more credible (*www.yokodana.com/testimonials.htm*, *www.zeus.com/customers/testimonials.html*; see Figures 5.15 and 5.16).

Visit www.theculturallycustomizedwebsite.com for additional information and updates.

CHAPTER KEYS

Countries fall at various points on the continuum of high uncertainty avoidance to low uncertainty avoidance.

To customize web sites on this value, the following can be incorporated to emphasize high uncertainty avoidance: customer service, guided navigation, tradition themes, local stores, local terminology, free trials or downloads, toll-free numbers, transaction security, and testimonials.

Thus, the higher the score a country has on uncertainty avoidance, the more relevant and important the above-mentioned web site characteristics become. For those countries at the low end of uncertainty avoidance, the above web site characteristics are not priorities; instead for these countries, the

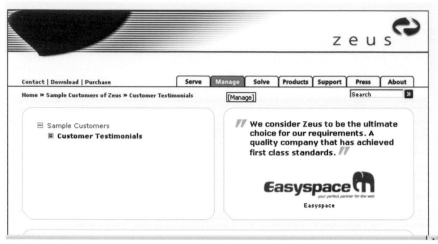

FIGURE 5.15 *www.zeus.com*

YokoTrading

Japanese Vintage Fabric & Garments, Ceremonial Kimono,
Specialty Pre-War Antiques & More Since 1989

| Catalog | Site Map | Home Page |

TESTIMONIALS

Dear Dana & Yoko...

I just got my 20 lb box of cotton kimono cloth. I am so happy!! I took one apart and I could not believe how much fabric there was. I love the selection you sent. It was exactly what I wanted. Thank you so much. And, I found a nice suprise in the box....a bolt of the most delicious cotton for kimono. I didn't expect that. You've won me over and I can't wait to work with these fabrics and to order more. I wish I could get 100 pounds!!! (hmmmmm maybe) There is one kimono in the box that is in such great condition that I think I'll give to my dad for father's day. I think he will like it very much. I will make a sash with some of the other kimono cloth to keep it closed. Again thank you and I'm so happy I decided to order. Domo arigatou!!!

Marguerite Cordice
Flushing, New York

Dear Dana,

Wow!
I got the package this afternoon.How should I describe after I went through all of them.It is too good to be true. Don't know how to express my satisfaction. Am I lucky! thank you.

Best regards,

FIGURE 5.16 *www.yokodana.com*

focus should be on those values (be they collectivism-individualism, power distance, masculinity-femininity, or high-low context) on which they have high scores.

EXERCISES

Students

1. In this chapter, we discuss the importance of blogs (weblogs) as a tool to present company employees as experts in specific areas of interest to customers. Visit the Jupiter Research web site (weblogs.jupiterresearch.com/ analysts) and see how this company is using blogs to position its analysts as experts in their fields. Create your own blog. It can be a fun exercise to create a forum with you as an expert in any area you are passionate about. There are several resources available to create blogs on the web. One such resource is *www.blogger.com/start*.

2. Search the Web and identify web sites that use a breadcrumb trail (one example is *www.southshropshire.gov.uk/static/page609.htm*).

Managers

Analyze any international web site targeted at a country high on uncertainty avoidance, and see if the features highlighted in this chapter are effectively implemented and leveraged to customize the site to the local audience. If you manage such a site, see if the suggestions in this chapter can be used in your print and other forms of communications targeted to cultures high on uncertainty avoidance.

REFERENCES

Gudykunst, W.B. (1998) *Bridging Differences: Effective Intergroup Communication*, 3rd ed. Thousand Oaks, CA: Sage Publications.

Hofstede, G. (1980) *Culture's Consequences: International Differences in Work-Related Values*. Beverly Hills, CA: Sage Publications.

Hofstede, G. (1991) *Culture and Organizations: Software of the Mind*. London: McGraw-Hill.

Lin, C.A. (2001) Cultural Values Reflected in Chinese and American Television Advertising, *Journal of Advertising*, 30(4), 83–94.

Lynch, P.D., Kent, R.J., and Srinivasan, S.S. (2001). The Global Internet Shopper: Evidence from Shopping Tasks in Twelve Countries, *Journal of Advertising Research*, 43(1), 15–23.

Mooij, M. de (1998) *Global Marketing and Advertising. Understanding Cultural Paradoxes*. Thousand Oaks, CA: Sage Publications.

Mooij, M. de (2003) Consumer Behavior and Culture: Consequences for Global Marketing and Advertising, The Netherlands: Cross Cultural Communications Company.

Mueller, B. (1992) Standardization vs. Specialization: An Examination of Westernization in Japanese Advertising, *Journal of Advertising Research*, 32(1), 15–24.

Pollay, R.W. (1983) Measuring the Cultural Values Manifest in Advertising. In J.H. Leigh and C.R. Martin (eds.), *Current Issues and Research in Advertising*, 72–92. Ann Arbor: MI: University of Michigan Press.

Sackmary, B. and Scalia, L.M. (1999) Cultural Patterns of World Wide Web Business Sites: A Comparison of Mexican and U.S Companies, *Paper Presented at the Seventh Cross-Cultural Consumer and Business Studies Research Conference*, Cancun, Mexico.

Singh, N. and Baack, W. D. (2004) Studying Cultural Values on the Web: A Cross-Cultural Study of U.S. and Mexican Web Sites, *Journal of Computer Mediated Communication*, 9(4), *www.ascusc.org/jcmc/vol9/issue4/*

Singh, N. and Matsuo, H. (2004) Measuring Cultural Adaptation on the Web: A Study of U.S. and Japanese Websites, *Journal of Business Research*, 57(8), 864–872.

Singh, N., Zhao, H., and Hu, X. (2003) Cultural Adaptation on the Web: A Study of American Companies' Domestic and Chinese Web Sites, *Journal of Global Information Management*, 11(3), 63–81.

Straub, D., Keil, M., and Brenner, W. (1997) *Testing the technology acceptance model across cultures: A three country study, Information & Management*, 33, 1–11.

Zahedi, F., Van Pelt, W.V., and Sont, J. (2001) A Conceptual Framework for International Web Design, *IEEE Transactions on Professional Communication*, 44(2), 83–103.

6

CULTURAL CUSTOMIZATION: POWER DISTANCE

This chapter focuses on the cultural value of power distance *and provides guidelines for designing web sites that conform to this value.*

CHAPTER HIGHLIGHTS
POWER DISTANCE: IN BRIEF
POWER DISTANCE: COUNTRY SCORES
RESEARCH ON POWER DISTANCE
DESIGNING WEB SITES FOR POWER DISTANCE

POWER DISTANCE: IN BRIEF

Key Issue

A belief in authority and hierarchy (high power distance) versus the belief that power should be distributed (low power distance).

Countries High on Power Distance

Malaysia, Panama, Guatemala, Philippines, Mexico, Venezuela, and China (see page 113 for a comprehensive list of country scores).

Countries Low on Power Distance

Austria, Israel, Denmark, New Zealand, Ireland, and Norway (see page 113 for a comprehensive list of country scores).

Operationalizing Power Distance on the Web

Company Hierarchy Information: Information about the ranks of company personnel, information about organizational chart, and information about country managers.

Pictures of CEOs: Pictures of executives, important people in the industry, or celebrities.

Quality Assurance and Awards: Mention of awards won, quality assurance information, and quality certification by international and local agencies.

Vision Statement: The vision for the company, as stated by the CEO or top management.

Pride of Ownership Appeal: Depiction of satisfied customers, fashion statement for the use of product, and the use of reference groups to portray pride.

Proper Titles: Titles of the important people in the company, titles of the people in the contact information, and titles of people on the organizational charts.

Caveats

1. The cultural value of power distance is one of the five values in the Cultural Values Framework that addresses the *"behavioral"* component of culture. Each country is a unique blend of all of the relevant cultural values; as such, for true cultural customization, all relevant values must be included. Further, the other two components of culture, *perception* and symbolism (discussed in Chapter 2), must also be part of any attempt at cultural customization of a web site. The features listed here are based on the work of Singh, Zhao, and Hu (2003) and Singh and Matsuo (2004).

2. The higher the score a country has on power distance, the more relevant and important the above-mentioned web site features become. For those countries at the low end of power distance, the above web site characteristics are not priorities; instead for these countries, the focus should be on those values (be they collectivism-individualism, uncertainty avoidance, masculinity-femininity, or high-low context) on which they have high scores.

3. The above features, when emphasized in a web site, make the site more closely customized to the cultural value of power distance. It should be noted that such features might well be present in sites that are not attempting such customization; however, it is not the mere presence of these features that matters, but the degree to which they are emphasized in a web site.

POWER DISTANCE: COUNTRY SCORES

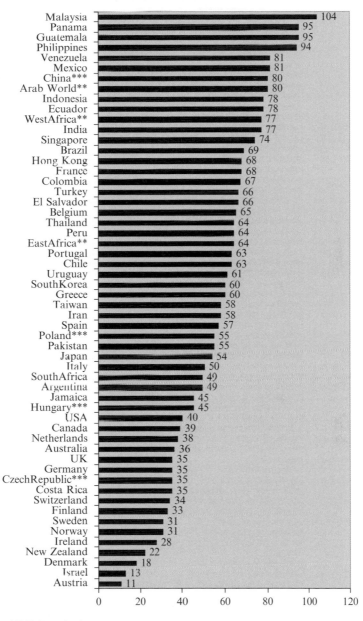

*** Estimated values
** *Arab World:* Egypt, Iraq, Kuwait Lebanon, Libya, Saudi Arabia, United Arab Emirates.
** *East Africa:* Ethiopia, Kenya, Tanzania, Zambia
** *West Africa:* Ghana, Nigeria, Sierra Leone
Source: Hofstede, G., *"Culture's Consequences: Comparing Values, Behaviors,
Institutions, and Organizations,"* Sage Publications, 2001.

FIGURE 6.1   Power Distance: Country Scores, Descending Order (High scores signify high power distance).

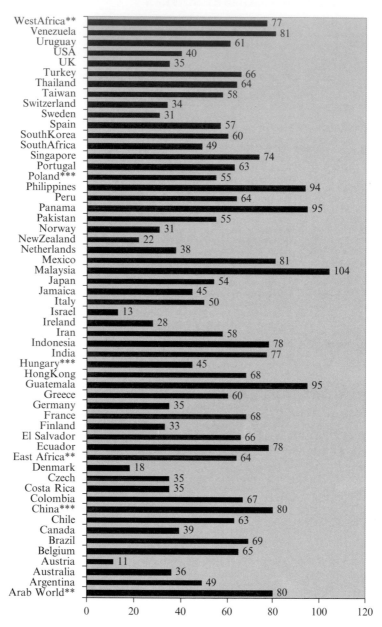

*** Estimated values
** *Arab World:* Egypt, Iraq, Kuwait Lebanon, Libya, Saudi Arabia, United Arab Emirates.
** *East Africa:* Ethiopia, Kenya, Tanzania, Zambia
** *West Africa:* Ghana, Nigeria, Sierra Leone

Source: Hofstede, G., *"Culture's Consequences: Comparing Values, Behaviors,
Institutions, and Organizations,"* Sage Publications, 2001.

FIGURE 6.2 Power Distance: Country Scores, Alphabetized Order (High scores signify high power distance).

RESEARCH ON POWER DISTANCE

The power distance dimension measures the extent to which a society accepts social hierarchy, social inequalities, and authority in the social system (Hofstede 1980). Countries high on power distance dimension tend to have a more hierarchical social structure, emphasize status and referent power, and value authority and legitimacy. On the other hand, countries low on power distance tend to be more egalitarian, accept less social hierarchy, and value equal rights for all.

People in high power distance societies tend to be very sensitive with regard to respect and obedience to the elderly and authority figures. For example, the Chinese are highly influenced in their purchase decisions by opinion leaders and authority figures (Ji and McNeal, 2001); a study by Mueller (1987) of Japanese advertisements showed extensive use of status appeal. In the case of both Japan and India, which are high power distance societies, the method of greeting, interacting, and even addressing a person is determined by the social status of the person (Mooij 2003). In such high power distance societies, individuals may show deference to authority by refraining from using media that do not allow them face-to-face contact (Straub et al. 1997, p. 4). So the question is how do we depict status, hierarchical structure, and personal authority on the web, which is a virtual medium with practically no direct human contact? To effectively target consumers in high power distance societies, companies need to find ways to let customers know the status of the people or company they are dealing with, status associated with the product or services they are selling, and how well respected the company is in the target country.

DESIGNING WEB SITES FOR POWER DISTANCE

Features that can help the web sites depict a high power distance orientation include the following described below (Singh and Baack, 2004; Singh and Matsuo, 2004; Singh, Zhao, and Hu 2003; Singh et al. 2004).

Hierarchy Information and Pictures of Important People

High power distance societies emphasize hierarchical structures and stress coercive and referent power (Gudykunst 1998; Hofstede 1991). In such cultures, written communications contain references to status and authority (Mooij 1998; Zahedi, Van Pelt, and Sont 2001). Moreover, people tend to obey recommendations from authority figures. For example, the Chinese are highly influenced in their purchasing by opinion leaders and authority figures (Ji and McNeal 2001; Yau 1988). The importance of hierarchical relationships in Chinese society can be traced back to Confucius's five cardinal relations between sovereign and minister, father and son, husband and wife, old and young, and friends (Ji and McNeal 2001). Japanese corporate web sites in comparison to Anglo, Nordic, or German web sites have been shown to greatly emphasize messages from the CEO and organizational charts (Robbins and Stylianou 2003). Information about the ranks of company personnel, organizational charts, information about country managers, pictures of CEOs and other important people, executive bios, and any other information that can help a customer to easily ascertain the status of the people associated with the company are all ways to depict a high power distance orientation on the web site. In both Japanese and Indian businesses, people place great importance to the rank and position of the person they are dealing with and then accordingly structure their greetings, behavior, and association. Given the inability of physical and personal interaction on the web site, photographs of important people in the company help customers get to know them and also help establish their basis for authority. For example, the Seven Eleven web site of Japan (*www.sej.co.jp/english/company/message.html*) prominently depicts the pictures of its CEO and COO and includes a brief message (Figure 6.3). These pictures of the Seven Eleven company's Chairman and President have an authoritative feel and present these people as powerful figures in the company.

A good example of an organizational chart is provided by Mexican company FEMSA's web site (*www.femsa.com/qsomos_sub.asp?sub_id<org*), wherein there is an elaborate organizational tree clearly showing people's rank and importance in the company (Figure 6.4). The web site of an Indian company, Mphasis (Figure 6.5; *www.mphasis.com/about_us/aboutus_execteam.asp*), also portrays the organizational structure of the company in three sections; namely, the executive team, board, advisory team and associates, and business partners.

FIGURE 6.3   *www.sej.co.jp*

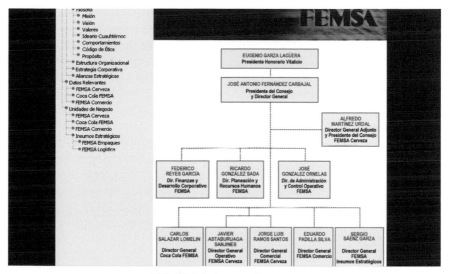

FIGURE 6.4 *www.femsa.com*

FIGURE 6.5 *www.mphasis.com*

Proper Titles

Societies that value status and hierarchy extensively use proper titles to clarify the status of the person in the society (Trompenaars 1994). In India, last names of people are frequently used to determine what their caste is, which part of the country they are from, and what Indian dialect they speak; furthermore, it is common to use words such as *Shri* (or *Sri*) and *Shrimati* to denote respect when addressing individuals. Similarly, Malaysia, which has the highest power distance score in the world, also uses titles to distinguish societal and cultural groups in the country. Many Malaysians have titles given to them by Malaysian royalty titles, such as *Datuk*, *Tan Sri*, and *Puan Seri*. In Mexico too, titles have an important role in determining and establishing people's status, and generally people with professional degrees are not addressed as *Señor* or *Señora*, but as *Licenciado*, *Ingeniero*, *Arquitecto*, and *Doctor*. Several Mexican web sites prominently display titles of important company people. In addition to plain titles, Mexican web sites also emphasize the professional degree the person holds. Thus, it is important to highlight proper titles of the people in the organization and use the titles to delineate individuals' positions in the corporate hierarchy. Titles of the important people in the company, titles of the people in the contact information, and titles of people on the organizational charts are just some ways to do this.

Quality Assurance and Awards

As people in high power distance societies value referent power, they stress popularity and recognition themes (Pollay 1983). Awards, certifications, and recognitions convey that the company's products are recognized by the society as being superior. Therefore, certifications, awards, and prizes are viewed as symbols of universal recognition in high power distance societies. Prominent display of quality, awards, and company recognition information are common on web sites of high power distance cultures. For example, the Brazilian web site *www.submarino.com.br* (Figure 6.6) has a dedicated gallery where pictures, details, and names of the awards won by the company are prominently shown (*www.submarino.com.br/local/home_premios.asp*).

Similarly, award, quality, and certification information is also very popular on most Indian web sites. An Indian company, Hero Honda Ltd. (Figure 6.7), chronologically lists all the awards, certifications and accolades it has won since 1991 (*www.herohonda.com/site/investors/index.asp?Sec<Awards+%26amp%3B+Accolades*).

Listing of awards and certifications to show status is not the only strategy followed by companies from high power distance countries. Companies also emphasize their superior quality and status link on their web sites. For example, Tata Tea Ltd. of India puts emphasis on its quality products and brands on its web sites (Figure 6.8) and positions itself as a superior quality tea brand *www.tatatea.com/quality.htm*.

Vision Statement

High power distance societies are characterized by autocratic and paternalistic tendencies, and conformity to the leader's views is encouraged (Hofstede

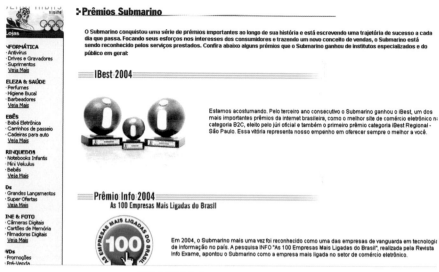

FIGURE 6.6 *www.submarino.com*

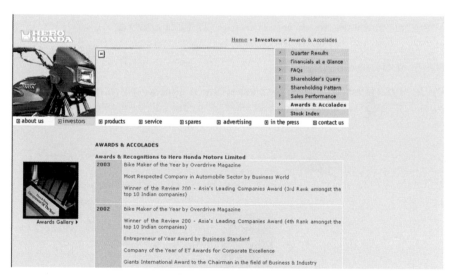

FIGURE 6.7 *www.herohonda.com*

1980). Thus, vision statements help people understand the philosophy of the top management. Several Japanese, Malaysian, Indian, and Mexican web sites prominently depict their vision statement or a statement from the CEO. For example, the Seven Eleven web site for Japan has a statement from its CEO, along with the CEO's picture. Other examples of high power distance

FIGURE 6.8   *www.tatatea.com*

country web sites include *www.cantv.com.ve/seccion.asp?pid<1&sid<168* from Venezuela and www.herohonda.com from India (Figures 6.9, 6.10).

Pride of Ownership Appeal

Pride of Ownership appeal emphasizes status appeal, which is valued in high power distance societies (Hofstede 1991; Mueller 1987). For example, Mueller

FIGURE 6.9   *www.cantv.com*

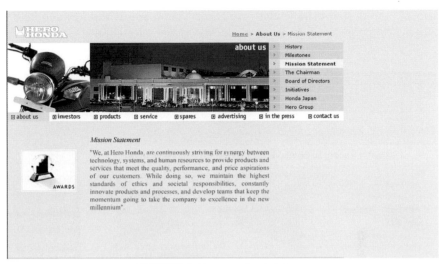

FIGURE 6.10   *www.herohonda.com*

(1987) found that Japanese advertisements emphasized status appeal. The status appeal is reflected in the form of product usage that bestows a higher status, or provides a particular, sought-after image for the consumer. This is further reinforced by advertising and product positioning strategies and the use of reference groups. Indonesia is high on power distance, and status appeal is reflected on several of its web sites. For example, the Indonesian web site *www.gmi-sukses.com* shows pride of ownership appeal on the home page with people of high status and a punch line stating the song "We are the champions, no time for losers" (Figure 6.11). Advertising in India tends to incorporate innuendos, appeals, and symbols that directly or indirectly link the brands to status and pride of ownership. Hero Honda, an Indian auto company, has a team of "brand Ambassadors," who are celebrities in India lending the Hero Honda brand a high status appeal (Figure 6.12; *www.herohonda.com/site/advertising/index.asp?Sec<Brand+Ambassadors*).

Visit www.theculturallycustomizedwebsite.com for additional information and updates.

CHAPTER KEYS

Countries fall at various points on the continuum of high power distance to low power distance.

To customize web sites on this value, the following can be incorporated to emphasize high power distance: company hierarchy information, pictures of CEOs, quality assurance and awards, vision statement, pride of ownership appeal, and proper titles (Singh and Baack 2004; Singh and Matsuo 2004; Singh, Zhao, and Hu 2003; Singh et al. 2004).

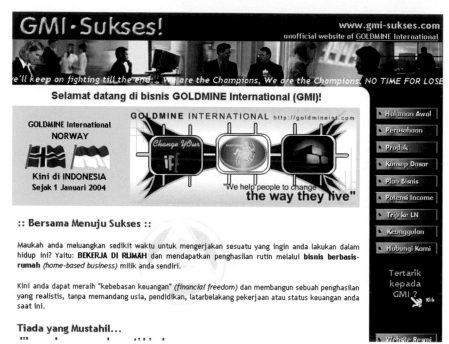

FIGURE 6.11   *www.gmi-sukses.com*

FIGURE 6.12   *www.herohonda.com*

Thus, the higher the score a country has on power distance, the more relevant and important the above-mentioned web site characteristics become. For those countries that are at the low end of power distance, the above web site characteristics are not priorities; instead for these countries, the focus should be on those values (be they collectivism-individualism, uncertainty avoidance, masculinity-femininity, or high-low context) on which they have high scores.

EXERCISES

Students

Visit the Indian web site of Hero Honda Motors Ltd., *www.herohonda.com/ site/home/home.asp*, and analyze how power distance features discussed in this chapter are depicted on the web site. The web site is in English; however, it uses local terminology from time to time, which is a feature characteristic of uncertainty avoidance.

Managers

Visit *local* (i.e., domestic) Malaysian, Mexican, and Indian web sites (some are in English, you can also use Goggle's language tools to machine translate the pages that require translation). See how these cultures that are high on power distance display this value through their web communications. Compare and contrast these local sites with those of sites of multinationals that target these countries.

REFERENCES

Gudykunst, W.B. (1998) *Bridging Differences: Effective Intergroup Communication*, 3rd ed. Thousand Oaks, CA: Sage Publications.

Hofstede, G. (1980) *Culture's Consequences: International Differences in Work-Related Values*. Beverly Hills, CA: Sage Publications.

Hofstede, G. (1991) *Culture and Organizations: Software of the Mind*. London: McGraw-Hill.

Ji, M.F. and McNeal, J.U. (2001) How Chinese Children's Commercials Differ from Those of the United States: A Content Analysis, *Journal of Advertising*, 30(3), 80–92.

Mooij, M. de (1998) *Global Marketing and Advertising: Understanding Cultural Paradoxes*. Thousand Oaks, CA: Sage Publications.

Mooij, M. de (2003) *Consumer Behavior and Culture: Consequences for Global Marketing and Advertising*, The Netherlands: Cross Cultural Communications Company.

Mueller, B. (1987) Reflections of Culture: An Analysis of Japanese and American Advertising Appeals, *Journal of Advertising Research*, 27(3) (June/July), 51–59.

Pollay, R.W. (1983) Measuring the Cultural Values Manifest in Advertising. In J.H. Leigh and C.R. Martin (eds.), *Current Issues and Research in Advertising*, 72–92. Ann Arbor: MI: University of Michigan Press.

Robbins, S.S. and Stylianou, A.C. (2003) Global Corporate Web Sites: An Empirical Investigation of Content and Design, *Information and Management*, 40(3), 205–212.

Singh, N. and Baack, W. D. (2004) Studying Cultural Values on the Web: A Cross-Cultural Study of U.S. and Mexican Web Sites, *Journal of Computer Mediated Communication*, 9(4), *www.ascusc.org/jcmc/vol9/issue4/*

Singh, N. and Matsuo, H. (2004) Measuring Cultural Adaptation on the Web: A Study of U.S. and Japanese Websites, *Journal of Business Research*, 57(8), 864–872.

Singh, N., Zhao, H., and Hu, X. (2003) Cultural Adaptation on the Web: A Study of American Companies' Domestic and Chinese Web Sites, *Journal of Global Information Management*, 11(3), 63–81.

Singh, N., Zhao, H., and Hu, X. (2004) Analyzing the Cultural Content of Web Sites: A Cross-National Comparison of China, India, Japan, and U.S., *International Marketing Review*.

Straub, D., Keil, M., and Brenner, W. (1997) Testing the technology acceptance model across cultures: A three country study, *Information & Management*, 33, 1–11.

Trompenaars, F. (1994) *Riding the Waves of Culture: Understanding Diversity in Global Business*, New York: Irwin Professional Publishing.

Yau, H.M.O. (1988) Chinese Cultural Values: Their Dimensions and MarketingImplications, *European Journal of Marketing*, 22(5), 44–57.

Zahedi, F., Van Pelt, W.V., and Sont, J. (2001) A Conceptual Framework for International Web Design, *IEEE Transactions on Professional Communication*, 44(2), 83–103.

7

CULTURAL CUSTOMIZATION: MASCULINITY-FEMININITY

This chapter focuses on the cultural value of masculinity-femininity *and provides guidelines for designing web sites that conform to this value.*

CHAPTER HIGHLIGHTS

MASCULINITY-FEMININITY: IN BRIEF
MASCULINITY-FEMININITY: COUNTRY SCORES
RESEARCH ON MASCULINITY-FEMININITY
DESIGNING WEB SITES FOR MASCULINITY-FEMININITY

MASCULINITY-FEMININITY: IN BRIEF

Key Issue

A belief in achievement, assertiveness, and ambition (masculine) versus a belief in nurturing and caring for others (feminine).

Countries High on Masculinity

Japan, Hungary, Austria, Venezuela, Switzerland, Italy, and Mexico (see page 127 for a comprehensive list of country scores).

Countries High on Femininity

Sweden, Norway, the Netherlands, Denmark, Costa Rica, Finland (see page 127 for a comprehensive list of country scores).

Operationalizing Masculinity on the Web

Quizzes and Games: Games, quizzes, fun stuff to do on the web site, tips and tricks, recipes, and other such information.

Realism Theme: Less fantasy and imagery on the web site, to-the-point information.

Product Effectiveness: Durability information, quality information, product attribute information, and product robustness information.

Clear Gender Roles: Separate pages for men and women, depiction of women in nurturance roles, depiction of women in "traditional" positions of telephone operators, models, wives, and mothers; depiction of men as macho, strong, and in positions of power.

Operationalizing Femininity on the Web

During the various research studies that form the basis for this book, we found that that the key aspects of femininity that can be operationalized on web sites are shared by the cultural value of high-context (see Chapter 8). They are the soft-sell approach and aesthetics and harmony.

Soft-Sell Approach: Use of affective and subjective impressions of intangible aspects of a product or service, and more entertainment themes to promote the product.

Aesthetics: Attention to aesthetic details, liberal use of colors, bold colors, emphasis on images and context, and use of love and harmony appeal.

Caveats

1. The cultural value of masculinity-femininity is one of the five values in the Cultural Values Framework that addresses the "*behavioral*" component of culture. Each country is a unique blend of all of the relevant cultural values; as such, for true cultural customization, all relevant values must be included. Further, the other two components of culture, *perception* and *symbolism* (discussed in Chapter 2), must also be part of any attempt at cultural customization of a web site. The features listed here are based on our previous research (Singh and Baack 2004; Singh and Matsuo 2004; Singh, Zhao, and Hu 2003).

2. The above features, when emphasized in a web site, make the site more closely customized to the cultural values of masculinity or femininity. It should be noted that such features may well be present in sites that are not attempting such customization; however, it is not the mere presence of these features that matters, but the degree to which they are emphasized in a web site.

MASCULINITY-FEMININITY: COUNTRY SCORES

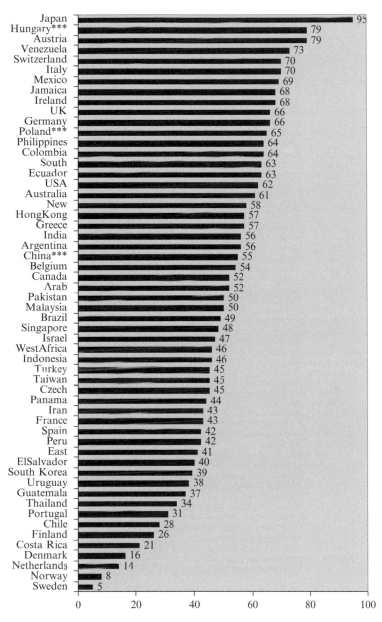

Japan 95
Hungary*** 79
Austria 79
Venezuela 73
Switzerland 70
Italy 70
Mexico 69
Jamaica 68
Ireland 68
UK 66
Germany 66
Poland*** 65
Philippines 64
Colombia 64
South 63
Ecuador 63
USA 62
Australia 61
New 58
HongKong 57
Greece 57
India 56
Argentina 56
China*** 55
Belgium 54
Canada 52
Arab 52
Pakistan 50
Malaysia 50
Brazil 49
Singapore 48
Israel 47
WestAfrica 46
Indonesia 46
Turkey 45
Taiwan 45
Czech 45
Panama 44
Iran 43
France 43
Spain 42
Peru 42
East 41
ElSalvador 40
South Korea 39
Uruguay 38
Guatemala 37
Thailand 34
Portugal 31
Chile 28
Finland 26
Costa Rica 21
Denmark 16
Netherlands 14
Norway 8
Sweden 5

*** Estimated values

** *Arab World:* Egypt, Iraq, Kuwait Lebanon, Libya, Saudi Arabia, United Arab Emirates.

** *East Africa:* Ethiopia, Kenya, Tanzania, Zambia

** *West Africa.* Ghana, Nigeria, Sierra Leone

Source: Hofstede, G., *"Culture's Consequences: Comparing Values, Behaviors, Institutions, and Organizations,"* Sage Publications, 2001.

FIGURE 7.1 Masculinity-Femininity: Country Scores, Descending Order (Higher scores signify masculinity).

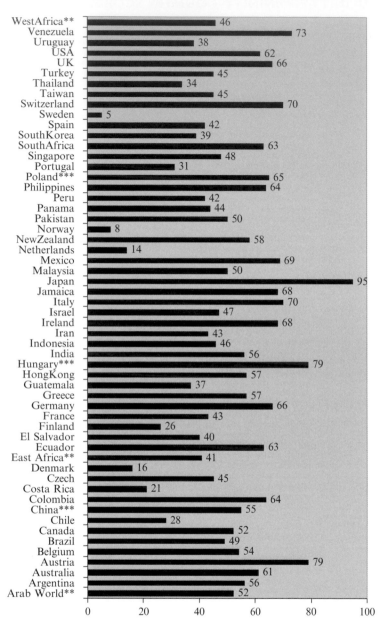

*** Estimated values
** *Arab World:* Egypt, Iraq, Kuwait Lebanon, Libya, Saudi Arabia, United Arab Emirates.
** *East Africa:* Ethiopia, Kenya, Tanzania, Zambia
** *West Africa:* Ghana, Nigeria, Sierra Leone

Source: Hofstede, G., *"Culture's Consequences: Comparing Values, Behaviors, Institutions, and Organizations,"* Sage Publications, 2001.

FIGURE 7.2 Masculinity-Femininity: Country Scores, Alphabetized Order (Higher scores signify masculinity).

RESEARCH ON MASCULINITY-FEMININITY

The masculinity-femininity dimension proposed by Hofstede (1980) explains how gender roles are allocated in different cultures, and what emphasis is placed on values like achievement, assertiveness, mastery, harmony, and caring. Masculine cultures value assertiveness, ambition, success, and performance. In such cultures, big and fast are admired, the masochism ideal is acceptable, and clear gender roles are the norm. Masculinity is commonly expressed in the form of success-orientation, admiration for strength, and clear gender role differentiation. On the contrary, "feminine" cultures value beauty, nature, nurturance, and blurred gender roles. In feminine countries, emphasis is placed on harmony, service-orientation, consensus, and modesty. Countries like Japan, Austria, Mexico, Germany, India, Australia, United Kingdom, and the United States are examples of masculine cultures, while most of the Nordic countries, Denmark, and the Netherlands score high on femininity. Appeals emphasizing a product's superior performance and capacity to accomplish goals are common in masculine cultures (Cheng and Schweitzer 1996). Masculine cultures are direct, decisive, and emphasize mastery over nature (Hofstede 1980); unlike feminine cultures, they are less inclined toward fantasy, imagery, and oneness with nature. Countries high on masculinity also tend to clearly communicate distinct gender roles for men and women. Marketing material in masculine countries tends to show men more in positions of control or power and women in secondary roles. Moreover, marketers in masculine countries tend to portray a masculine image for products targeted to men (Singh and Matsuo 2004; Singh, Zhao, and Hu 2003).

DESIGNING WEB SITES FOR MASCULINITY

When designing web sites for masculine countries, attributes such as success, performance, realism, fun/entertaining, adventure, and clear gender roles need to be incorporated in the web sites. The following discussion shows how these values can be highlighted on web sites (Singh and Baack 2004; Singh and Matsuo 2004; Singh, Zhao, and Hu 2003, 2004).

Product Effectiveness

In masculine cultures achievement, performance, and growth are emphasized (Gudykunst 1998; Hofstede 1991). Product durability, performance, and quality are emphasized in performance appeals (Albers-Miller and Gelb 1996). Appeals emphasizing a product's superior performance, speed and strength, and capacity to accomplish goals are common in masculine cultures (Cheng and Schweitzer 1996). Advertisements commonly depict such product performance, service performance appeals in masculine countries. For example, studies show that advertising appeals in masculine cultures are more task-oriented or success-oriented, with emphasis on product performance. German commercials for detergents argue performance of the detergent by emphasizing the piles of dirty clothes that a housewife can wash using the detergent, depicting the woman as an effective housewife rather than as a caring mother (Mooij 1998). Similarly, on the web site of the German automobile manufacturer BMW, the car is positioned as "The Ultimate Driving Machine," and phrases depicting performance appeal are common: "Part Athlete, Part Genius, All BMW," "No one ever said civilized had to ever mean tame," "Any weather, Any corner, Any pace, Any Passion," "Jack of all trades, Master of all roads." Performance, quality, and product effectiveness also have important advertising appeal in Japan, which scores highest on masculinity. For example, Olympus Corporation of Japan positions itself as tough, effective, and high performing by aligning itself with a sports car like Ferrari. Olympus was the official sponsor of Ferrari at the Grand Prix circuits in 2003, and a high-profile advertisement campaign was launched to associate Olympus with this event. The objective of the campaign was to link power, excitement, and speed of the Formula 1 race with the high photographic performance of Olympus cameras (see Figure 7.3; *www.olympus.co.jp/en/magazine/pursuit/200402/html/f_article.html*). Thus, to depict this performance appeal on web sites, companies need to use graphics and pictures showing success, winning, quality, and performance and elaborate on product durability information, quality information, product attribute information, and product robustness information.

FIGURE 7.3   *www.olympus.com*

Quizzes and Games

Advertising in masculine cultures emphasizes the basic value of enjoyment (Pollay 1983), and reflects adventure themes, thrills and games, and success-orientation (Cheng and Schweitzer 1996; Mooij 1998). For example, as mentioned earlier, Olympus uses the fun and excitement of the Formula 1 race to position its products as high performance. The Olympus web site also has web pages dedicated to fun stuff like "Tips and tricks," "Meet the Pros," "Online lessons," "Photo contests," and so on. Such material is sometimes presented in a separate area called "the coffee break section," which is generally set up to help bored or fatigued online consumers to relax on the web site and have fun. These sections are filled with games, cartoons, contests, and other interesting information. For example, the Japanese site of Nissan has a special section on amusement that offers screen savers, wallpaper, and other items. Another example is the Indian web site, Hindustan Lever (Figures 7.4, 7.5), which promotes a shampoo called Clinic and has a whole section devoted to online games (*www.clinicallclear.com/games.htm*). Thus, to make the web sites more fun, exciting, and success-oriented, it is important to include features such as games, quizzes, tips and tricks, recipes, and other similar material.

FIGURE 7.4 *www.clinicallclear.com*

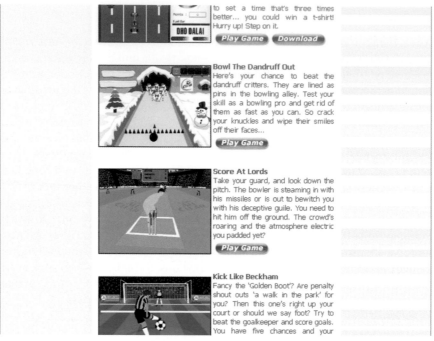

FIGURE 7.5   *www.clinicallclear.com*

Realism Theme

As masculine cultures are direct, decisive, and emphasize mastery over nature (Hofstede, 1980), they are less inclined toward fantasy, imagery, and oneness with nature appeals. Masculine cultures favor toughness and value material that is pragmatic and appropriate (Albers-Miller and Gelb 1996; Zahedi, Van Pelt, and Sont 2001). Less fantasy and imagery on the web site, to-the-point information, and use of rational or performance appeals are common. Performance and quality takes precedence over fantasy and entertaining themes. A neat, simple, less cluttered, and effective site of the German company Falk esolutions (*www.falkag.de/index1.htm*) is an example of the realism theme being used (see Figure 7.6). On this site the phrase, "your right choice" is frequently used to depict in a simple but effective way their quality and performance. On their American web site, Falk e-solutions prominently uses the phrase, "The Internet is so fast that the present is often the past. We'll show you the future," depicting performance appeal.

Clear Gender Role

In masculine societies, gender roles are clearly differentiated, and men dominate in most market settings (Hofstede 1991). Clear gender role differentiation is vis-

FIGURE 7.6 *www.falkag.de*

ible in advertising in different cultures. It is common to see women depicted in familial situations and associated with distinct feminine roles in masculine societies. On the other hand, men are portrayed as macho and depicted as important and powerful. In masculine cultures, depictions of father-son or mother-daughter combinations are more prevalent, while in feminine cultures, pictures of father-daughter or mother-son are not uncommon (Mooij 1998). For example, Figure 7.7 shows a picture of a mother and daughter in front of a Seven Eleven store in Japan (*www.sej.co.jp*). Figure 7.8 shows a father-son combination on the web site of the German company, Henkel (*www.henkel.com*).

The Excite search engine for Japan has a separate section or engine capability dedicated to Japanese women, depicting clear role differentiation in the masculine Japanese society. The Woman Excite web site (Figure 7.9; *woman.excite.co.jp*) has sections like beauty, lifestyle, food, love, career, horoscope, travel, and others. Another Japanese company, Toshiba, has a special section for women (Figure 7.10; *feminity.toshiba.co.jp/feminity/index2.html*), which has products addressing the needs of Japanese women. There is an exclusive Arab web site dedicated to Arab female teens, *www.banateen.com*, which has three main sections for teen girls on mind, body, and soul. These sections are filled with things like clubs, chats, forums on teen issues, horoscope, beauty, food, and so on (Figure 7.11). On several Japanese, Chinese, Mexican, and Arabic web

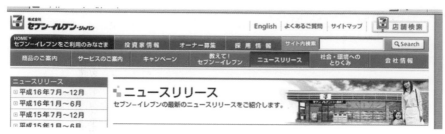

FIGURE 7.7 *www.sej.co.jp*

FIGURE 7.8 *www.henkel.com*

FIGURE 7.9 *www.excite.co.jp*

FIGURE 7.10   *www.toshiba.co.jp*

sites, women are shown as mothers, wives, customer service representatives, and models, whereas men are shown in important company positions, company pictures, as executives on-the-go, and in other positions of power. Thus, to design sites for masculine cultures, clear gender role differentiation is important. This can be accomplished by creating separate pages for men and women, in which women are depicted in nurturance roles, in customer service positions, and as models, wives, and mothers, and men are depicted as macho and strong, doing manual work, and as powerful personalities. (*Note: We are not advocating or judging the obvious stereotypical issues inherent in the above discussion; we are just reporting the existing cultural practices in masculine culture.*)

DESIGNING WEB SITES FOR FEMININITY

As described at the beginning of the chapter, the key elements of femininity that can be operationalized on a web site are shared with the cultural value of high-context (see Chapter 8). Discussion of these elements (aesthetics and harmony and soft-sell) are provided in the next chapter.

Visit www.theculturallycustomizedwebsite.com for additional information and updates.

CHAPTER KEYS

Countries fall at various points on the continuum of high masculinity to high femininity.

FIGURE 7.11   *www.banateen.com*

To customize web sites on this value, the following can be incorporated to emphasize masculinity: quizzes and games, realism theme, product effectiveness, and clear gender roles.

To emphasize femininity, web sites must incorporate aesthetics and harmony, and a soft-sell approach to marketing their products.

EXERCISES

Students

Visit the web site of MTV India (*www.mtvindia.com/*) and see how MTV is using contests, fun stuff, and a heavy emphasis on "Bollywood" (the Indian film industry) to lure Indian youth, who are from a masculine culture. Note the level of celebrity emphasis on the site (including film stars, sports figures, as well as VJs), and the use of yellow and orange color in the site; these colors are considered sacred in India.

Managers

Study and analyze the *local* (i.e., domestic) country web sites in your industry for highly masculine countries like Japan, Germany, Mexico, Italy, and others. This exercise will help you see how such cultures depict masculinity value on their web sites. Then use the categories discussed in this chapter to help you implement the features that you would like to emphasize on your web site targeted to masculine cultures.

REFERENCES

Albers-Miller, N.D. and Gelb, B.D. (1996) Business Advertising Appeals as Mirror of Cultural Dimensions: A Study of Eleven Countries, *Journal of Advertising*, 25(Winter), 57–70.

Cheng, H. and Schweitzer, J.C. (1996) Cultural Values Reflected in Chinese and U.S Television Commercials, *Journal of Advertising Research*, (May/June), 27–45.

Gudykunst, W.B. (1998) *Bridging Differences: Effective Intergroup Communication*, 3rd ed. Thousand Oaks, CA: Sage Publications.

Hofstede, G. (1980) *Culture's Consequences: International Differences in Work-Related Values*. Beverly Hills, CA: Sage Publications.

Hofstede, G. (1991) *Culture and Organizations: Software of the Mind*. London: McGraw-Hill.

Mooij, M. de (1998) *Global Marketing and Advertising: Understanding Cultural Paradoxes*. Thousand Oaks, CA: Sage Publications.

Pollay, R.W. (1983) Measuring the Cultural Values Manifest in Advertising. In J.H. Leigh and C.R. Martin (eds.), *Current Issues and Research in Advertising*, pp. 72–92. Ann Arbor: MI: University of Michigan Press.

Singh, N. and Baack, W. D. (2004) Studying Cultural Values on the Web: A Cross-Cultural Study of U.S. and Mexican Web Sites, *Journal of Computer Mediated Communication*, 9(4), *www.ascusc.org/jcmc/vol9/issue4/*

Singh, N. and Matsuo, H. (2004) Measuring Cultural Adaptation on the Web: A Study of U.S. and Japanese Websites, *Journal of Business Research*, 57(8), 864–872.

Singh, N., Zhao, H., and Hu, X. (2003) Cultural Adaptation on the Web: A Study of American Companies' Domestic and Chinese Web Sites, *Journal of Global Information Management*, 11(3), 63–81.

Singh, N., Zhao, H., and Hu, X (2004) Analyzing the Cultural Content of Web Sites: A Cross-National Comparison of China, India, Japan, and U.S., *International Marketing Review*, (in press).

Zahedi, F., Van Pelt, W.V., and Sont, J. (2001) A Conceptual Framework for International Web Design, *IEEE Transactions on Professional Communication*, 44(2), 83–103.

8

CULTURAL CUSTOMIZATION: HIGH-LOW CONTEXT

This chapter focuses on the cultural value of high-low context and provides guidelines for designing web sites that conform to this value.

CHAPTER HIGHLIGHTS

HIGH-LOW CONTEXT: IN BRIEF
HIGH-LOW CONTEXT: COUNTRY CATEGORIES
RESEARCH ON HIGH-LOW CONTEXT CULTURES
DESIGNING WEB SITES FOR HIGH CONTEXT CULTURES
DESIGNING WEB SITES FOR LOW CONTEXT CULTURES

HIGH-LOW CONTEXT: IN BRIEF

Key Issue

In high context cultures and their communication style, most information is embedded in the context or internalized among the members of the society. In low context cultures, messages are straightforward, detailed, and explicitly coded in unambiguous terms.

High Context Countries

In general, countries in Asia, Africa, South America, and much of the Middle-East are classified as high context. More specifically, Japan, China, Korea, Malaysia, Indonesia, Thailand, Taiwan, the Philippines, Turkey, France, Italy, Spain, Portugal, and Greece are all high context countries (in random order).

Low Context Countries

In general, much of Northern Europe and North America is classified as low context. Specifically, Australia, New Zealand, Austria, Canada, Scandinavia, Germany, the United States, Switzerland, and the United Kingdom are all low context countries (in random order).

Operationalizing High Context on the Web

Politeness and Indirectness: Greeting from the company, images and pictures reflecting politeness, flowery language, use of indirect expressions (e.g., "perhaps," "probably," "somewhat"), and overall humility in company philosophy and corporate information.

Soft-Sell Approach: Use of affective and subjective impressions of intangible aspects of a product or service and use of entertainment theme to promote the product.

Aesthetics: Attention to aesthetic details, liberal use of colors, bold colors, emphasis on images and context, and use of love and harmony appeal.

Operationalizing Low Context on the Web

Hard-Sell Approach: Aggressive promotions, discounts, coupons, and emphasis on product advantages using explicit comparison.

Use of Superlatives: Use of superlative words and sentences like "We are number one," "The top company," "The leader," "World's largest."

Rank or Prestige of the Company: Features like company rank in the industry, listing or ranking in important media (e.g., Forbes, Fortune, etc.), and numbers showing the growth and importance of the company.

Terms and Conditions of Purchase: Product return policy, warranty, and other conditions associated with the purchase.

Caveats

1. The cultural value of high-low context is one of the five values in the Cultural Values Framework that addresses the "*behavioral*" component of culture. Each country is a unique blend of all of the relevant cultural values; as such, for true cultural customization, all relevant values must be included. Further, the other two components of culture, *perception* and *symbolism* (discussed in Chapter 2), must also be part of any attempt at cultural customization of a web site. The features listed here are based on Singh, Zhao, and Hu (2003), Singh and Baack (2004), and Singh and Matsuo (2004).

2. The above features, when emphasized in a web site, make the site more closely customized to the cultural values of high or low context. It should be noted that such features might well be present in sites that are not attempting such customization; however, it is not the mere presence of these features that matters, but the degree to which they are emphasized in a web site.

HIGH-LOW CONTEXT: COUNTRIES

High Context	Low Context
Japan	Australia
China	Austria
Korea	Canada
Malaysia	Germany
Indonesia	U.S.A.
Thailand	U.K.
Taiwan	New Zealand
Philippines	Switzerland
Turkey	Denmark
Greece	Netherlands
France	*Scandanavia*
Italy	*N. America*
Spain	*N. Europe*
Portugal	
S. America	
Africa	
Middle-East	

FIGURE 8.1   High-Low Context Country Classification (in random order).

RESEARCH ON HIGH-LOW CONTEXT CULTURES

As individuals, we act and communicate within a context. This context is, to an extent, provided by the meanings we attach to words, symbols, values, acts, and other elements of the contextual environment. According to Hall (1976), we cannot act or communicate in any meaningful way except through the medium of culture. Culture provides the context, which is rich in meaning, values, symbols, and nonverbal elements that are difficult to decipher holistically for a person not belonging to that culture. Hall (1976) provides us with a cultural dimension that can help us to understand how people in different cultures communicate in their daily lives. To communicate effectively across cultures, the correct level of context has to be found. This context can be labeled as high or low, on a sliding scale. High context societies have close connections among group members, and everybody knows what every other person knows. Thus, in such cultures or societies, much of the information to function in a group is intrinsically known, and there is little information that is explicit, or transmitted as part of the message. High context cultures use more symbols and nonverbal cues to communicate and most of the meanings are embedded in the situational context. Thus, emphasis is more on symbols and clues in the environment (Singh, Zhao, and Hu 2003). According to Cho et al. (1999), advertising in high context cultures emphasizes harmony, beauty, and oneness with nature (Cho et al. 1999). Advertisements in high context cultures are characterized by indirect verbal expressions and are implicit, indirect, polite, modest, and even ambiguous (Mooij 1998; Mueller 1987). Direct comparisons are not viewed favorably (Mueller 1987).

Low context cultures are societies that are logical, linear, and action-oriented, and the mass of the information is explicit and formalized. Most of the communication in such cultures takes place in a rational, verbal, and explicit way to convey concrete meanings through rationality and language. People in such cultures use precise words to convey meanings, and the message is often received literally, with less reliance on nonverbal clues. Thus, the use of direct, explicit, and confrontational appeals in the form of advertising and promotions, as well as aggressive selling, is common in such cultures (Cutler and Javalgi 1992). Mueller (1987) found that low context cultures such as the United States make explicit mention of competitor products and emphasize a hard-sell orientation. Low context cultures emphasize clear communication and rely less on the unspoken context (Singh and Matsuo 2004).

Scandinavia is classified on the low context end of the High and Low context dimension. This is visible in several Scandinavian web sites that depict simplicity, clarity in communication, less hodgepodge of content, non-aggressive tone, and succinctness. (Figures 8.2–8.4).

FIGURE 8.2   *www.autodb.no*

FIGURE 8.3   *www.spele.nl*

FIGURE 8.4   *www.huuto.net*

DESIGNING WEB SITES FOR HIGH CONTEXT CULTURES

The following paragraphs elaborate what elements need to be emphasized to culturally adapt to cultures that are high context (Singh and Baack 2004; Singh and Matsuo 2004; Singh, Zhao, and Hu 2003, 2004); two of the elements (aesthetics and soft-sell) are also relevant in the case of the "feminine" aspect of the masculinity-femininity value (see Chapter 7).

Aesthetics

A study by Cho et al. (1999) found that communications in high context cultures tend to emphasize harmony and beauty. The use of symbols and icons in the form of art, designs, beautiful scenery, festivals, and nature appeals is common (Gudykunst 1998; Mueller 1987, 1992). Symbols and icons become specifically important when communication elements are embedded in the context. Japan is considered as one of the high context cultures where substantial information is embedded in the context surrounding the message. Thus, the use of symbols, art-forms, and other iconic expressions is common in Japanese communication style. Symbols and icons serve as a conduit of intrinsic meanings and messages that need not be conveyed verbally. Japanese love for beauty and aesthetics is captured in two words: *shibui*, which refers to the quality of the beauty, and *mono-no-aware*, which symbolizes a merging of one's consciousness with an object's beauty (Gannon 1994). For example, pictures of butterflies, cherry blossoms, other nature scenes, and cultural artifacts are commonly seen on Japanese web sites (Singh, Zhao, and Hu 2004), epitomizing *shibui* and *mono-no-aware*. These elements of nature on Japanese web sites also symbolically convey the harmony between nature and man. Japanese society values group harmony (given that it is a collectivist society), and nature symbolism is commonly used to express this harmony in human relations (Gannon 1994). Similarly, Chinese web sites frequently use color symbolism, icons, and cultural symbols like dragons, pagodas, Chinese architecture, the Great Wall, festivals, and other visual metaphors symbolizing harmony (Singh, Zhao, and Hu 2004). The Chinese view harmony in the form of *Yin* and *Yang*; *Yin* is viewed as feminine, dark, cool, and passive, while *Yang* is seen as male, light, and warm. Chinese use this concept frequently in their lives to achieve balance. It is also reflected in the choice of colors, which should blend in harmony. Thus, it is important to choose colors that complement each other in the form of *Yin* and *Yang* and depict overall harmony on the web site. The importance of harmony in Chinese culture can be seen in numerous prayers for harmony on walls, doorsteps, charms, and even wedding cakes (Gannon 1994). An example of a web site depicting Chinese symbolism and harmony is shown in Figure 8.5 (*www.avl.com.cn/avl2y/cardindex.htm*), which shows auspicious dragons and liberal use of red and gold depicting happiness and power, respectively. Thus, when designing web sites for high context cultures, attention needs to be paid to aesthetic details, liberal use of colors, high bold colors, emphasis on images, symbols and context, and use of harmony appeal.

Politeness and Indirectness

Advertisements in high context cultures are characterized by indirect verbal expressions, and communication through messages is implicit, indirect, polite, modest, and even ambiguous (Lin 1993; Miracle, Chang, and Taylor 1992;

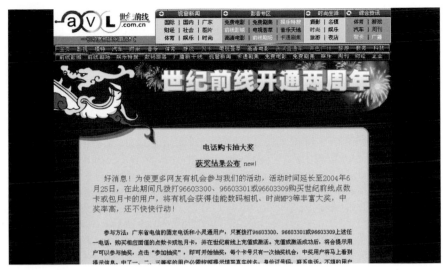

FIGURE 8.5 *www.avl.com*

Mooij 1998). Direct comparisons are not viewed favorably (Mueller 1987). Advertisements in such cultures attempt to be polite, with the objective of establishing a friendly relationship with a viewer or reader of the advertisement. Thus, Japanese advertisements have been shown to depict subtlety and modesty (Mueller 1987). Japanese web sites also depict politeness in the form of customary notes of thanks to the customers, greetings to the customers, and notes of best wishes for good health, all items not commonly seen in web sites of low context cultures like the United States and Germany. The web sites of Hitachi and Fujitsu show a general feel of courtesy and harmony in the form of liberal use of expressions about harmony and co-existence. Middle-East and South Asian countries, also high context cultures, have an extensive vocabulary that specifically accommodates words that convey politeness. For example, Urdu, a language commonly spoken in Pakistan and parts of India, is considered one of the most polite languages; it uses various words to emphasize politeness and respect. The English word "you" can be translated into three similar words in Urdu: *"Tu," "Tum,"* and *"Aap." Aap* is the most courteous way to address a person. Thus, politeness can be emphasized on web sites targeted for high context cultures by including greetings from the company, images and pictures reflecting politeness, flowery language, and the use of indirect words like "perhaps," "probably," and "somewhat."

Soft-Sell Approach

Advertisements in high context cultures tend to have a soft and more emotion-based appeal; advertising tends to be more suggestive than direct (Cho et al.

1999). Emotions, sentiments, and entertainment themes are emphasized over clear-cut direct appeals (Mueller 1987, 1992). The emphasis in the advertisements is on subtle linking of company product to place, person, event, or symbol to convey the sales pitch. Moreover, the sales pitch is subdued, uses fewer words and more images and symbols, and makes implicit claims rather than explicit claims of product superiority. The soft-sell approach is reflected in Chinese and Japanese advertising via a modest decorum in the sales pitch, less verbally aggressive expressions, and an overall modesty in tone (Lin 1993; Mueller 1987). Such advertising is also seen in France, which is a high-context culture. The French web site of Sodexho Corporation, a company in the business of food and management services, is an example of a web site designed for high context cultures (Figure 8.6; *www.sodexho.com/SodexhoAnglais/ detect.cfm*). This web site is colorful and sells its services indirectly using the entertainment and harmony theme. The web site is not divided into company, product, and service information, but uses more subtle expressions to convey the same information. The web site has sections like, "A time for greeting," "A time for living," "A time for knowing," "A time for initiating," and "A time for understanding."

Thus, features like the use of affective and subjective impressions of intangible aspects of a product or service and more entertainment and symbolic themes to promote the product can help culturally adapt to high context cultures.

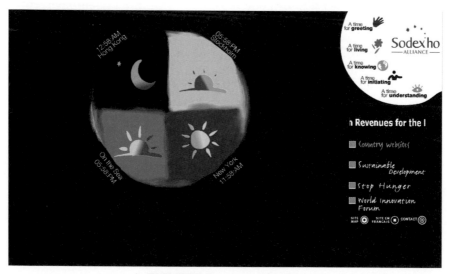

FIGURE 8.6 *www.sodexho.com*

DESIGNING WEB SITES FOR LOW CONTEXT CULTURES

The following paragraphs elaborate what elements need to be emphasized to culturally adapt to low context cultures (Singh and Baack 2004; Singh and Matsuo 2004; Singh, Zhao, and Hu 2003; Singh, Zhao, and Hu 2004).

Terms and Conditions

Low context cultures emphasize clarity, background information, and directness. The information is vested in explicit code (Hall 1976). Thus, advertisements and communications in such cultures tend to be informative (Cho et al. 1999). In the United States, it is common to see products advertised with reams of fine print detailing legal and product information, so as to explicitly communicate with the customers and secure against lawsuits that may arise from incomplete information. Such need for detailed information and procedures is not common in high context cultures where trust, product safety, and performance are assumed as a part of an established brand name. Almost all American web sites have a section at the bottom of the home page detailing terms and conditions for the use of its products and information on the web site. Thus, it is important to clearly make visible to consumers the product return policy, warranty, and other conditions associated with the purchase.

Hard-Sell Approach

Communications in low context cultures are direct, explicit, and even confrontational (Hall 1976). Thus, use of direct and confrontational appeals in the form of advertising, aggressive sales promotions, and "hard" selling is common in such cultures (Cutler and Javalgi 1992). Mueller (1987) found that low context cultures like the United States make explicit mention of competitor products and emphasize sales orientation. Appeals in such cultures emphasize rational arguments and are more verbose than symbolic. For example, the German BMW web site has a special section on shopping tools where it makes rational arguments to convince you to view BMW cars favorably and even compare BMW cars with those of the competition. Similarly, there is also a proliferation of shopping bots (a bot is intelligent software that searches the Web to find comparative product offerings) that specialize in comparative shopping (e.g., *www.mysimon.com*; see Figure 8.7). Comparative advertising, though popular in low context cultures like United States, is illegal in some Asian countries.

The use of aggressive promotions (deals, discount, special promotions) is commonly seen in low context cultures like the United States and the United Kingdom; aggressive promotions are less prevalent in high context cultures.

FIGURE 8.7   *www.mysimon.com*

Rank or Prestige and Use of Superlatives

Advertisements in low context cultures also use implicit comparisons to highlight the benefits and the prestige of the products and the company brand (Mueller 1987). Statements such as "the number one company" and "the leader of the industry" "the best," or "the number one" are common. The tone of communication in such cultures is direct and rhetorical in style (Caillat and Mueller 1996). Thus, aggressive communication style and use of superlatives is common; in fact, in low context cultures like the United States, it is pervasive at every level, be it a small town bagel restaurant (*www.worldsbestbagels.com*) or an internet marketing company (*www.trafficmp.com/trafficmp/home/home.asp*) (Figures 8.8, 8.9).

Visit www.theculturallycustomizedwebsite.com for additional information and updates.

CHAPTER KEYS

High context and low context are the polar opposites of the same cultural value, and various countries fall on this continuum, depending on their contextual tendencies.

If the country of interest is predominantly high -context, a web site can be adapted to conform to this value by incorporating the following: politeness and indirectness, a soft-sell approach, and aesthetics.

If the country of interest is predominantly low context, the following can be incorporated into a web site: a hard-sell approach, use of superlatives, rank or prestige of the company, and terms and conditions of purchase.

FIGURE 8.8   *www.worldsbestbagels.com*

FIGURE 8.9   *www.trafficmp.com*

EXERCISES

Students

Compare two local Japanese (high context) web sites and two local American (low context) web sites from any industry (e.g., the travel industry) and see if you find differences on the following characteristics: politeness and indirectness, a soft-sell approach, and aesthetics (all high context features) and a hard-sell approach, use of superlatives, rank or prestige of the company, and terms and conditions of purchase (all low context features).

Managers

Choose a web site that targets a high (or low) context country (e.g., *www.amazon.jp*). Select a successful local competitor's web site from that same country (e.g., any successful Japanese online book retailer.) Analyze the two web sites on every relevant feature discussed in this chapter.

Analyze your print and television advertising to see if you are leveraging the concept of high and low context cultures to the fullest and try to extend this cultural dimension to your web communications.

REFERENCES

Caillat, Z. and Mueller, B. (1996) The Influence of Culture on American and British Advertising: An Exploratory Comparison of Beer Advertising, *Journal of Advertising Research*, 36(3), 79–87.

Cho, B., Kwon, U., Gentry, J.W., Jun, S., and Kropp, F. (1999) Cultural Values Reflected in Theme and Execution: A Comparative Study of U.S. and Korean Television Commercials, *Journal of Advertising*, 28(4), 59–73.

Cutler, B.D. and Javalgi, R.S.G. (1992) A Cross-Cultural Analysis of Visual Components of Print Advertising: The United States and European Community, *Journal of Advertising Research*, 32(Jan/Feb), 71–80.

Gannon, M.J. and Associates (1994) *Understanding Global Cultures*. Thousand Oaks, CA: Sage Publications.

Gudykunst, W.B. (1998) Bridging Differences: *Effective Intergroup Communication*, 3rd ed. Thousand Oaks, CA: Sage Publications.

Hall, E.T. (1976) *Beyond Culture*. Garden City, NY: Doubleday.

Lin, C.A. (1993) Cultural Differences in Message Strategies: A Comparison between American and Japanese TV Commercials, *Journal of Advertising Research*, 33(4), 40–49.

Miracle, G.E., Chang, K.Y., and Taylor, C.R. (1992) Culture and Advertising Executions: A Comparison of Selected Characteristics of Korean and U.S. Television Commercials, *International Marketing Review*, 9(4), 5–17.

Mooij, M. de (1998) *Global Marketing and Advertising: Understanding Cultural Paradoxes*. Thousand Oaks, CA: Sage Publications.

Mueller, B. (1987) Reflections of Culture: An Analysis of Japanese and American Advertising Appeals, *Journal of Advertising Research*, 27(3)(June/July), 51–59.

Mueller, B. (1992) Standardization vs. Specialization: An Examination of Westernization in Japanese Advertising, *Journal of Advertising Research*, 32(1), 15–24.

Singh, N. and Baack, W. D. (2004) Studying Cultural Values on the Web: A Cross-Cultural Study of U.S. and Mexican Web Sites, *Journal of Computer Mediated Communication*, 9(4), *www.ascusc.org/jcmc/vol9/issue4/*.

Singh, N. and Matsuo, H. (2004) Measuring Cultural Adaptation on the Web: A Study of U.S. and Japanese Websites, *Journal of Business Research*, 57(8), 864–872.

Singh, N., Zhao, H., and Hu, X. (2003) Cultural Adaptation on the Web: A Study of American Companies' Domestic and Chinese Web Sites, *Journal of Global Information Management*, 11(3), 63–81.

Singh, N., Zhao, H., and Hu, X. (2004) Analyzing the Cultural Content of Web Sites: A Cross-National Comparison of China, India, Japan, and U.S., *International Marketing Review*, *www.emeraldinsight.com*.

9

CULTURAL CUSTOMIZATION: THE FUTURE IS HERE

This chapter discusses the present and future of cultural customization and the associated long-term rewards of such customization and offers concluding thoughts.

CHAPTER HIGHLIGHTS

CULTURAL CUSTOMIZATION: HERE TO STAY
"BORN GLOBAL": IMPLICATIONS FOR CULTURAL CUSTOMIZATION
CONCLUDING THOUGHTS
RESOURCES

CULTURAL CUSTOMIZATION: HERE TO STAY

The relentless march of globalization has brought with it profound and far-reaching effects. We are presently witnessing an unprecedented migration of peoples across the world, the erasing and redefining of national borders, and the instantaneous flow of information. All these factors have profound effects on people's sense of identity, allegiance, loyalty, and most important to businesses, their patterns of consumption and purchase behavior.

More to the point of this book, they affect people's perception and behavior vis-à-vis web sites and their purchase behavior therein. Thus, even as this book makes a practical case for using *countries* as a basis for *culture*, and the customization of web sites based on countries (see Preface and Chapter 3), what does the future hold? Will cultural customization of web sites based on countries be valid in a world where the ultimate effects of globalization could well be global customers with global identities, with little allegiance and loyalty to their own cultures and countries? The answer, based on a recent research study (Singh et al. 2004), is a cautious yes.

The concept of a global identity has been defined as a world-mindedness value orientation that emphasizes a sense of belongingness, empathy, and sharing with humankind as a whole (Sampson and Smith 1957). National identity has had various conceptualizations, such as a national consciousness or an attitude related to a sense of affiliation, common fate, and kinship to one's nation state (Der-Karabetian and Balian 1992; Der-Karabetian and Ruiz 1997; Zak 1973). Globalization and its effects can be argued to affect both global identity and national identity. In fact, these two identities are not polar opposites, but rather can co-exist side by side. In other words, people can be "high" on both global *and* national identity (as well as low on both, or a combination of high and low). Singh et al. (2004) show that in all four combinations of global and national identity (high global, high national; high global, low national; low global, high national; low global, low national), the relevance of cultural customization of web sites *does exist*. These results indicate that people's global identity and cultural background will continue to impact their attitude toward cultural customization of web sites. In fact, there is evidence that with global convergence, people are increasingly holding on to their national and cultural identity, cherishing and supporting it. As such, cultural customization of web sites is seemingly *here to stay*.

Such a long-term expectation of the importance of cultures makes for an even stronger case for the cultural customization of web sites. We believe that there will be long-term rewards for those who invest in comprehensive cultural customization of web sites, after having clearly identified the relevant customer segments. This is depicted in the top extreme right box of Figure 9.1. As Figure 9.1 illustrates, defining your target market but doing little more than offering a standardized web site or limited customization (i.e., minimal customization, such as a translated web site) will likely lead to lost opportunities and limited success, respectively.

	No Customization	Limited Customization	Cultural Customization
Defined Segments (e.g.countries)	Lost Opportunity	Limited Success	Long-term Success
Undefined Segments	Potential Failure	Wasted Resources	Wasted Resources

GLOBAL CUSTOMER SEGMENTATION

WEBSITE CUSTOMIZATION

FIGURE 9.1   Global Segments and Web Site Customization.

"BORN GLOBAL": IMPLICATIONS FOR CULTURAL CUSTOMIZATION

Cultural customization must be accomplished at the very inception of the web site. Web sites may not have the luxury of building their customer base incrementally, one segment at a time. Web sites are "born global," and if they are not ready at their launch to attract the various targeted customers, they may never do so. This is because an online visitor may never come back to a web site if, on his or her first visit, the web site does not suit his or her needs. More important, if that visitor is part of a targeted segment, not only is a potential customer lost, but also lost is the opportunity to attract other likely customers through word of mouth recommendations. As such, web sites must be culturally customized to attract every customer segment targeted, right at their launch.

To do so, companies must first identify their international segments (typically countries), and second, identify the make-up of the country's culture in terms of the five cultural values discussed in this book and review the relevant issues of perception and symbolism (discussed in Chapter 2) for that culture.

Resources needed to achieve successful cultural customization include money, time, manpower commitment, working with a localization agency, departmental coordination to compile the content, dedicated personnel to coordinate cultural customization globally, and a vision to tap into the vast global online markets. The input from foreign subsidiaries or local offices (if available) can be extremely important when developing web content that is culturally customized for a target market.

It is not sufficient just to develop culturally customized web sites; it is also important that targeted customers find it easy to locate the web sites. Thus, global gateways become an important part of an effective global web site (Yunker 2003). Global gateway or landing pages help to bring all Web users to a common platform from where they can select their country of interest and be directed to a local web site. In this context, many web sites make the mistake of having their home pages in English and providing links to their international web sites—making the tenuous assumption that all international online users are fluent in English. For example, Lexmark International (*www.lexmark.com*) has a global gateway page (Figure 9.2), which lists the country web site links, but both the names of the countries and the content on the page are in English. Similarly Levi's (*www.levi.com*) has a global gateway or landing page (Figure 9.3), but all the world regions and links to specific countries are in English. Another example, Visa International (*www.visa.com/globalgateway*) shows a map of the world (Figure 9.4) on which you can click to find your country; however, the content is in English.

A global gateway should have minimal language-specific content; it can be possibly designed to show the different sites on a world map or have a simple chart or graphic with each country name spelled in the relevant native lan-

FIGURE 9.2 *www.lexmark.com*

FIGURE 9.3 *www.levi.com*

guage. Some web sites with creative and effective global gateways include Ikea (*www.ikea.com*), 3Com (*www.3com.com*), and E-trade (*www.etrade.com*) (Figures 9.5 to 9.7). Ikea's global gateway has minimal written content, a graphic to affirm its brand identity, and a list of country web sites in both English and the official language of the country in question—all displayed prominently on the gateway.

Also relevant is the clear and prominent position of the various international links; it's not helpful to international customers to have the links to their web sites hidden in a corner of the bottom of the page. For example, the

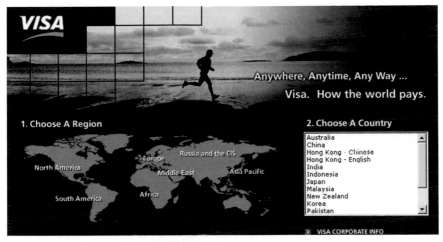

FIGURE 9.4   *www.visa.com*

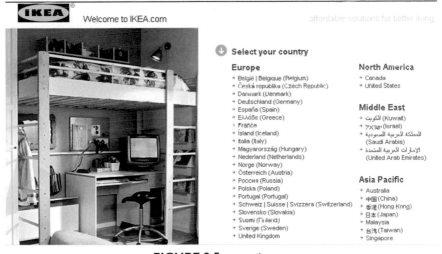

FIGURE 9.5   *www.ikea.com*

MTV home page has a link for its international web sites right at the bottom of its home page.

Beyond the various features (based on cultural values) discussed in this book, cultural customization of web sites must include an awareness of other key elements like currency conversion, logistics and shipping policy, legal issues, privacy issues, sales jurisdiction, customer care (for each country or at a centralized point), systems to effectively deal with customer feedback, and

SELECT A WEBSITE

Americas	Asia Pacific	Europe, Middle East & Africa
Brasil (Português)	Asia Pacific (English)	Benelux (Français)
Canada (English)	中国	Benelux (Nederlands)
Canada (Français)	日本	Central Europe (Deutsch)
Latinoamérica (Español)	한국	Česká A Slovenská Republika
United States	台湾	Danmark
		Europe (English)
		France
		ישראל
		Italia
		Middle East (Arabic)
		Middle East (English)
		Norge
		Polska
		Россия
		Spain
		Suomi
		Sverige
		United Kingdom & Ireland

For a list of 3Com offices worldwide click here.

FIGURE 9.6   *www.3com.com*

E✱TRADE
FINANCIAL®

Start Here   Select your location and preferred language:

Customer log on

User Name:	Password:

Country & Language:
United States - English ▾   **LOG ON**

🇺🇸 United States	English 中文 Deutsch
🇦🇺 Australia	English
🇨🇦 Canada	English Français
🇩🇰 Danmark	Danmark
🇩🇪 Deutschland	Deutsch English
🇭🇰 Hong Kong	繁體中文 English
🇯🇵 Japan	日本文
🇰🇷 South Korea	한국어 English
🇸🇪 Sverige	Sverige
🇬🇧 United Kingdom	English

FIGURE 9.7   *www.etrade.com*

customer concerns that might be in any world language that is targeted, time and date formatting, and order forms that are customized to country-specific writing styles in terms of name, address, and zip codes, and appropriate measurement scales.

CONCLUDING THOUGHTS

The book focused on the five cultural values individually (Chapters 4–8); however, it must be noted that ultimately, countries are an amalgamation of the five cultural values, which blend together to produce a unique national culture, along with aspects of perception and symbolism (discussed in Chapter 2). Thus, *www.real.com* (Figure 9.8) is an example of a web site that displays the American cultural values of individualism ("freedom of choice" as well as low context [the aggressive and direct comparison to competition.]) As such, each country is a complex mix of the values, even if they start with the individual values. For example, both Germany and Japan lean toward masculinity and are high on uncertainty avoidance and power distance; however, in the case of Japan, their collectivism combined with high context creates a distinct configuration of values that sets Japanese culture apart from the German culture. Previous work on culture (Mooij 1998) shows that different cultural values intermingle to produce unique configurations of values; for example, the combination of weak uncertainty avoidance and masculinity creates a value structure where success, individual expression, and creativity are valued (e.g., in the United States). Similarly, if high uncertainty avoidance value is combined with individualism (as in the case of Germany), it is reflected in a communication style that is structured, explicit, and straightforward (low context), whereas if high uncertainty is combined with collectivism, it is reflected in a communication style that is rooted in tradition and relies on implicit rules and codes (high context) (Mooij 1998). Regardless of the end cultural identity of a country, its foundations lie in the five individual cultural

FIGURE 9.8 *www.real.com*

behavioral values discussed in this book, along with aspects of *perception* and *symbolism* (discussed in Chapter 2). As such, if you follow the recommendations in this book, you will be able to develop a culturally customized web site that will enable you to connect more closely with your targeted customers, which in turn will increase your potential for long-term success on the Web.

Visit www.theculturallycustomizedwebsite.com for additional information and updates.

RESOURCES

Web Sites

www.clickz.com/stats/: Internet Statistics and Demographics
www.lisa.org/: Localization industry standard association
lrc.csis.ul.ie/index.htm: Localization research center
www.emarketer.com/: A good source for current e-commerce (global) news
www.nua.ie/surveys/: Surveys, demographics, e-tools, global statistics, etc.
www.mit.edu/people/mkgray/net/: Internet Statistics
world.altavista.com/: Babel fish, a machine translator
www.alexa.com/: A resource for local and international web site rankings and traffic analysis
www.glreach.com/: Global online marketing resources
www.bytelevel.com/: Resource for web site globalization
www.idiominc.com/: Localization and translation service; some white papers
www.worldlingo.com/: A multilingual product provider; lots of language resources
www4.gartner.com/Init: Various e-commerce reports
www.yankeegroup.com/: National and international e-commerce reports
www.lionbridge.com/: A web globalization solution provider
www.welocalize.com/: Localization agency with cultural expertise
www.globalsight.com/: A localization agency with localization resources
www.etranslate.com/: A translation agency
www.uniscape.com/: E-business globalization solutions
www.lib.umich.edu/govdocs/stsci.html: Statistical information on e-commerce, e-government, and the Internet
www.wilsonweb.com: A massive collection of articles on various e-commerce issues, including web globalization
www.dhark.com/web_design.html: Web design and internationalization resource links
www.welocalize.com/: Localization agency; Internet market research reports and world statistics
www.unicode.org/: Site for Unicode standard that supports various world languages; great resource for developing multilingual pages

Books

Beyond Borders: Web Globalization Strategies: By John Yunker (New Riders, IN).

Designing User Interfaces for International Use: By Jacob Neilsen (Elsevier Science Publishing).

The Unicode Standard, Version 4.0: By the Unicode Consortium (Book News Inc.).

XML Internationalization and Localization: By Yves Savourel (SAMS Publishing).

A Practical Guide to Localization: By Bert Esselink (John Benjamins Publishing).

REFERENCES

Der-Karabetian, A. and Balian, N. (1992) Ingroup, Outgroup, and Global-Human Identities of Turkish-Armenians, *Journal of Social Psychology*, 132, 497–504.

Der-Karabetian, A. and Ruiz, Y. (1997) Affective Bicultural and Global-Human Identity Scales for Mexican-American Adolescents, *Psychological Reports*, 80, 1027–1039.

Mooij, M. de (1998) *Global Marketing and Advertising: Understanding Cultural Paradoxes.* Thousand Oaks, CA: Sage Publications.

Singh, N., Fassott, G., Chao, M., Hoffman, J. and Bartikowski, B. (2004) Impact of Global and National Identity on International Web Site Usage (Work in Progress). (Contact ncsingh@csuchico.edu for details.)

Sampson, D.L and Smith, H.P. (1957) A Scale to Measure World-Minded Attitudes, *Journal of Social Psychology*, 45, 99–106.

Yunker, J. (2003) *Beyond Borders: Web Globalization Strategies.* Indianapolis, IN: New Riders.

Zak, I. (1973) Dimensions of Jewish-American Identity, *Psychological Reports*, 33, 891–900.

INDEX